Leadership
and
Entrepreneurship

This book is one of a series titled **Entrepreneurship: Principles and Practices,** sponsored by the Center for Entrepreneurial Leadership Inc. of the Ewing Marion Kauffman Foundation. The series merges the experiences of successful entrepreneurs with the applied research of leading scholars. It seeks to combine the best practices of entrepreneurs with the relevant, useful and impactive findings of leading scholars. The series thus provides an opportunity to increase our understanding of the entrepreneurial process by focusing on the factors that help entrepreneurs succeed.

TITLES IN THE SERIES

Growing New Ventures, Creating New Jobs: Principles & Practices of Successful Business Incubation, by Mark P. Rice and Jana B. Matthews.

Leadership and Entrepreneurship

Personal and Organizational Development in Entrepreneurial Ventures

Edited by
Raymond W. Smilor and Donald L. Sexton

Entrepreneurship: Principles and Practices

Prepared under the auspices of the
Center for Entrepreneurial Leadership Inc.

QUORUM BOOKS
Westport, Connecticut • London

Library of Congress Cataloging-in-Publication Data

Leadership and entrepreneurship : personal and organizational
  development in entrepreneurial ventures / edited by Raymond W.
  Smilor and Donald L. Sexton.
        p.   cm.—(Entrepreneurship: principles and practices, ISSN
  1083–334X)
    Includes bibliographical references and index.
    ISBN 1–56720–043–5 (alk. paper)
    1. Industrial management.   2. Leadership.   3. Organizational
change—Management.   4. Entrepreneurship.   I. Smilor, Raymond W.
II. Sexton, Donald L.   III. Series.
HD31.L326   1996
658.4'092—dc20   95–41385
      "Prepared under the auspices of the Center for Entrepreneurial Leadership Inc."

British Library Cataloguing in Publication Data is available.

Library of Congress Catalog Card Number: 95–41385
ISBN: 1–56720–043–5
ISSN: 1083–334X

First published in 1996

Quorum Books, 88 Post Road West, Westport, CT 06881
An imprint of Greenwood Publishing Group, Inc.

Printed in the United States of America

The paper used in this book complies with the
Permanent Paper Standard issued by the National
Information Standards Organization (Z39.48–1984).

10 9 8 7 6 5 4 3

*This book is dedicated
to the memory of "Mr. K."
Ewing Marion Kauffman*

Contents

Illustrations

Preface

The intensity of worldwide competition, especially in the product price/cost area, has brought about a change in the American economy equivalent to that which occurred during the Industrial Revolution.

Reengineering, reorganization, and outsourcing occurring within large corporate organizations have provided opportunities for growth in emerging companies that are unparalleled in our nation's history. Larger firms are realigning their efforts to meet the needs of their customers. In some situations this means eliminating products and/or entire product lines, restructuring staff functions, and eliminating layers of management. In addition, many larger firms are outsourcing or subcontracting the production of subassemblies, products, or product lines to smaller firms. Cost benefits result from lower direct labor rates and the lower overhead costs of smaller firms that can produce the products at the desired level of quality and on a "just in time" delivery schedule.

Estimates of jobs expected to be eliminated at larger firms vary, but they tend to cluster around two million jobs per year for the next five to seven years, for a total of 10 to 14 million jobs.

Not all of these reductions mean that the unemployment rate will expand considerably. Some reduction in jobs will result from normal attrition and retirement incentives that do not impact on unemployment rates.

Many corporate jobs will be eliminated as production is transferred to smaller firms. Yet, the outsourcing will result in increased hiring among smaller firms in order to meet the increased demand for outsourced products by large firms.

In essence, the reengineering of large firms will result in a supply of qualified and knowledgeable people who will either join smaller firms or start their own businesses. In addition, retirement incentives or "golden handshakes" may also provide the funding required to establish a new business. Hence, the availability of qualified people and the increased demand for products and services provide a boon to those existing and "would be" businesses that are prepared to take advantage of the new opportunities.

With the opportunities that currently exist and those that are expected to become available in the next five to seven years, most analysts expect a significant increase in the number of firms growing at a rate of 15 percent per year or more. Currently, this group includes the 1.4 million companies that purchase 44 percent of all business products.

This is truly a remarkable period in the history of entrepreneurship. The entrepreneurial spirit is alive and well, and many emerging firms will become large corporations as a result of the changing economic conditions.

The current entrepreneurial revolution is expected to have a significant impact on the economic growth of the United States, resulting in a much larger number of midsize or emerging firms and a change in emphasis among policymakers as this segment responds to the changing needs of a national and a worldwide society.

What do we really know about these firms and their founders that enable them to join the ranks of what in the past was a relatively small number of fast growth firms? We know they have been largely ignored by government policymakers who seem to concentrate on large corporate organizations and small, newly initiated firms. These midsize, rapidly growing firms are too large to be considered small and too small to be considered large. Unfortunately, we know little about them—about what motivates them, how they pursue opportunities, and how they build and motivate their organizations to pursue opportunities and growth as a normal approach to doing business. What can we learn from these "movers and shakers" that will enable us to help others pursue opportunities in meaningful, effective, and ethical ways? Do they know secrets or "tricks of the trade" that others are unaware of? Or are they just lucky? We think not.

Entrepreneurs make their own luck by being prepared to pursue a growth opportunity and taking the risk to pursue it. Preparedness is a function of many things: one is a desire to grow; another is the capability to grow. The desire lies within the mind of the entrepreneur. It is a "can do" attitude that, when combined with skill and opportunity, leads to economic expansion.

What constitutes these attitudes and brings about the development of resources necessary to achieve growth? Inherent in resource accumulation and allocation is the recognition of people as a major resource. Consideration of this important resource, and its motivation and application to the problems of growing firms, is the key to expanding the capabilities of the founder. Further, such action assists in the transformation of the firm from dependence on an entrepreneurial leader to a purpose-driven, goal-oriented firm. To many, this is the key to growth and the primary emphasis of this book.

ACKNOWLEDGMENTS

It is a pleasure to thank friends and associates who contributed time and talent to this book and to the conference on which it is based.

We wish to especially acknowledge two exceptional organizations—the Center for Entrepreneurial Leadership Inc. (CEL) of the Ewing Marion Kauffman Foundation and the Henry W. Bloch School of Business and Public Administration at the University of Missouri-Kansas City. We appreciate the support and encouragement of Michie P. Slaughter, president of CEL, and William B. Eddy, dean of the Bloch School.

This volume is based on the conference, "Entrepreneurship and Leadership: Personal and Organizational Development in Entrepreneurial Ventures," which was held in Kansas City in October 1993. We are grateful to the planning committee, many of whom also serve on the Council for Entrepreneurship at the Bloch School, that shaped the program for this conference: William Eddy; Clifford Illig, president, Cerner Corporation; Peter K. Lemke, president, EFL Associates; Larry Maddox, general partner, Allsop Venture Partners; Jana Matthews, senior research and teaching fellow, CEL; Kurt Mueller, partner, Ernst & Young; Ted Murray, president, The Winbury Group; John Palmer, president, EDP Enterprises; Bradley P. Pemberton, partner, Polsinelli, White, Vardeman & Shalton; Richard Stilwell, president, SCG Management Consulting, Inc.; James B. Stowers, Jr., chief executive officer, Twentieth Century Companies, Inc.; and Richard C. Smith, Jr., senior vice president, Sprint research and teaching fellow, CEL. We particularly want to acknowledge the energy, expertise, and tremendous goodwill that the late Jack McCarthy brought to this group.

We thank Sandra Colyer and Linda Franta, of the Bloch School for their important help in organizing and running the conference, and are grateful to our associates at the Kauffman Foundation for their outstanding support and entrepreneurial spirit: Barbara Anderson, Kate Hodel, Pam Kearney, Pattie Mansur, Mary Miller, Alicia Mitchelson, and Patsy Neblock. The expert workshop facilitation of Dan Grace, human resources consultant; Marilyn Kourilsky, vice president, CEL; and Robert Sherwood, president, Center for Business Innovation; are appreciated very much.

We are grateful also to Andrea Warren who provided invaluable assistance in preparing the manuscript for publication and thank Quorum Books for their editorial support. Further, we appreciate the direction and entrepreneurial approach of James Sabin, executive vice president of Greenwood Publishing Group, Inc., in establishing the book series for which this is the second volume.

We have also benefited from the commitment and enthusiasm of the Board of Directors of the Center for Entrepreneurial Leadership Inc.: Michie P. Slaughter, Chairman and President, CEL Inc., Ewing Marion Kauffman Foundation; Bert Berkley, Chairman of the Board, Tension Envelope Corp.; Patricia M. Cloherty, President, Patricof & Co.; Robert Compton, General Partner, CID Equity Partners; Willie Davis, President and CEO, All-Pro Broadcasting; Paul Henson, Chairman of the Board, Kansas City Southern Industries; Michael F. Herman, Ewing Marion Kauffman Foundation; Robert B. Rogers, Chairman and CEO, Ewing Marion Kauffman Foundation; Louis Smith, President and COO, Ewing Marion Kauffman Foundation; and Jeffry Timmons, Harvard University and Babson College.

Finally, we thank the contributing authors for sharing their ideas, insights, and knowledge. Through their efforts, this book seeks to improve our understanding of the practice of entrepreneurship by weaving the experiences of successful entrepreneurs with the analysis of applied academics. It is our hope that this approach provides useful examples for entrepreneurs and new perspectives for scholars.

Introduction

Worldwide competition brought about by advances in information technology has resulted in major changes in the business climate. Pressure to compete on cost, service, and quality has resulted in a reengineering of the corporate world. Changes brought about by reengineering, such as corporate downsizing and outsourcing, have fed explosive growth within the relatively small number of fast growth firms that were poised to take advantage of opportunities.

The current entrepreneurial revolution can be described as "the best of times" for growth-oriented firms that are rising to meet the increased demand for lower-priced products and services, and as the worst and best of times for large corporate organizations. They are the worst of times as jobs are eliminated and products are subcontracted to lower cost but equal quality entrepreneurial firms. They will be the best of times when, based on the current changes, corporate America will once again be able to compete on price, quality, and service.

The growth being experienced by a relatively small number of firms is in part due to their lower production and administrative costs, their ability to manage these costs, their ability to identify opportunities in the marketplace, and their ability to muster the necessary resources to pursue these opportunities.

Effective marketing, financial management, operations management, and product development and design are important aspects of growth. But what unifies these functions to advance the goals of the firms is the entrepreneur and the entrepreneurial team.

Interest in the entrepreneur as a founder, leader, manager, and contributor to the economic base of a city, region, or country, and as one who shares the wealth of the endeavor with others, has resulted in research on why these people are so successful. Studies have considered psychological characteristics, education, lifetime experiences, and a number of other characteristics to explain why entrepreneurs do what they do.

In the following pages, the editors have taken a somewhat different approach, emphasizing what entrepreneurs do, how they do it, and what can be learned by examining the common themes or concepts that exist in the practice of entrepreneurship.

This book presents the expertise of participants in a conference on leadership and entrepreneurship that examined the entrepreneur from a personal, organizational, and multidimensional point of view. The conference brought together successful entrepreneurs from profit and not-for-profit firms, from hardware and software firms, and from manufacturing and service firms to join with assistance providers, academicians, and researchers in an effort to more fully learn, understand, and convey to others the aspects of leadership that contribute to success in growth-oriented firms.

Management of growth requires skills and abilities above and beyond those required in the management of firms that are not growing rapidly. Three of these skills and/or abilities are to effectively lead the organization, to shape and build the organization, and to build value into the organization. These three skill/ability dimensions form the outline of this book.

PERSONAL DIMENSIONS: THE ENTREPRENEUR AS A LEADER

Dennis Kimbro introduces the concept and problems of the entrepreneur as a leader through an examination of the entrepreneur's sense of urgency and passion for accomplishment. He also examines the vision and mission inherent in entrepreneurs and their understanding of success—which, along with financial rewards, includes doing something they want to do.

John Eggers and Raymond Smilor suggest that entrepreneurs must manage paradoxically and create change in an evolving world. Through a panies and presents seven keys to success, including hiring self-motivated people; helping each other to be successful; creating clarity in the organization; communicating your values and philosophies; providing an appropriate reward system; creating an experimental learning attitude; and celebrating your victories.

MULTIDIMENSION: BUILDING VALUABLE COMPANIES

This section examines ways of making the entrepreneurial team work, provides an understanding of enhancing the value of the firm, discusses the concept of building value through strategic alliances, and describes the problems and successes of strategic alliances in technology transfer applications.

Lee Bolman and Terrence Deal discuss the need to change leadership styles to keep up with changes throughout the world. They use Microsoft's competition with IBM as a case study of how new leadership styles can work. To them, effective leadership requires a clear focus, an effective structure, and high performance expectation. With these come a sense of ownership, a contribution, and a desire for achievement.

Robert Kuhn discusses techniques for increasing the dollar value of the company by viewing the company from the eyes of a prospective buyer. He advises that formulas do not accurately predict the value of a business, and that value is in the eyes of the buyer and is based on both recent performance and future potential. His five steps for preparing a business for sale are avoiding long pay-back investments, planning for organizational success, altering the company's financial management, resolving the big issues, and adjusting the product mix.

Jana Matthews suggests that strategic alliances and partnerships can offer substantial benefits to both entrepreneurial companies and large companies. She also suggests using a value chain assessment to help select the best partners and a series of actions to evaluate how well the partners work together and whether or not the partnership should be maintained.

Finally, Edward Payne discusses some of the problems encountered by a new company formed to transfer technology to a firm at which the principals knew nothing about the technology. After a series of trials and tribulations, a value chain approach was utilized to develop the needed strategic alliances for introducing an innovative new product to the marketplace.

significant research study, they examine the need for different leadership styles as an organization grows. They also conclude that although common themes can be found in successful management of growth, it is often impossible to predict which venture will succeed.

Ewing Kauffman's insights on building the uncommon company came from interviews and presentations made before his death. His management style was based on two key principles: those who produce should share in the profits, and treat others as you would be treated. Kauffman believed that success and happiness would come from sharing your profits and treating people as you would be treated.

The final chapter in this section is one in which Neal Patterson shares the "pearls" of wisdom he received from Mr. Kauffman and how that advice has guided his activities in building Cerner into a large and successful firm. As with Mr. K, Patterson's recipe for successful leaders is to work hard and have fun.

ORGANIZATIONAL DIMENSION: SHAPING THE ENTREPRENEURIAL ORGANIZATION

William Davidow examines today's entrepreneurial leaders by projecting the reader 30 years into the future and looking back at the decade of the 1990s to see what can be learned from the current explosion of technology and its future impact. He suggests that the company of the future will be a virtual firm that is heavily dependent on information products that are easily adaptable to the needs of the user.

Jack Stack suggests that an open-book approach to management, in which all employees are aware of the financial aspects of the firm, allows employees to be fully aware of their individual impact on profitability and, therefore, recognizes all employees as managers of the firm's assets. Stack's view of management's role is to cheerlead and keep everyone on target. The result is a strong sense of unity and a "can do" environment where people work their hardest and have fun doing it.

Robert Rosen suggests that healthy people make healthy companies, and that healthy companies have the best chance of being profitable. He provides six principles to the creation of a healthy company, including the power of respect is greater than the power of money; wise leaders know how to follow; if you don't manage change, it will manage you; and healthy people are assets that appreciate in value.

Michie Slaughter draws upon his experience in building successful com-

REMAINING ISSUES AND NEEDS

Taken together, the chapters in this book provide a look at "best practices" in leadership and entrepreneurship from a personal and organizational perspective. The book includes chapters prepared by successful entrepreneurs, assistance providers, and researchers in an effort to build theory based on reality. We hope that this brief look at the phenomenon called entrepreneurship will whet the appetite of others to look, learn, practice, and contribute to the body of knowledge in this exciting field.

Part 1

Personal Dimension: The Entrepreneur as a Leader

Mission, Vision, and Passion in the Entrepreneur

Dennis P. Kimbro

When you knock on opportunity's door, you better make sure your bags are packed.

Dennis Green, NFL coach

If you are not a millionaire or bankrupt by your thirtieth birthday, you're not really trying!

Nolan Bushnell, founder of Atari

I've begun everything with the idea that I could succeed, and I never had much patience with those who were always ready to explain why I couldn't.

Booker T. Washington, educator

When the vision is clear, nothing else matters.

Wally Amos

I relinquished everything for the dream.

John H. Johnson

Entrepreneurs share in common a sense of urgency and a passion for accomplishment. They attempt things others won't, and they do things first. So many entrepreneurs have succeeded in the United States that in Europe this phenomenon is called "the American miracle." What differences can we see between the entrepreneurs who succeed and those who fail?

Successful entrepreneurs have vision, mission, and passion. They also understand what success actually is, and that success, like happiness, lies within us. They are the individuals who have experienced the greatest personal growth. Doing something important and something that pleases them is as important to them as money.

Successful entrepreneurs have a clear, focused vision. They keep their imaginations free and they translate them into words and action. They are also filled with passion, burning with a competitive desire to excel and win. If the passion for what you are doing is not there, then do something else.

Entrepreneurs also have a desire for independence, a sense of purpose, tolerance of uncertainty, perseverance, self-esteem, salesmanship, and self-discipline. Finally, they are willing to work hard and know that there are no short cuts. Success rarely comes overnight.

Few of us think of Malcolm X, the celebrated Muslim minister, as an entrepreneur. But he once told fellow entrepreneur Percy Sutton, founder of Inner City Broadcasting, "We should give life our best. Let us use our lives more wisely to chase our dreams, embrace a vision, and be as happy and successful as possible."

Malcolm X lived by those words, and so do other successful entrepreneurs, all of whom share in common a sense of urgency and a passion for accomplishment. They skate on the visionary edge. They attempt things other won't and they do things first. They have the ability to see an opportunity where others see chaos and confusion. They are impassioned men and women who accept risk and uncertainty in exchange for independence, freedom, and potentially high rewards.

Entrepreneurs learn from the past, while living in the present—with one eye on the future. According to Timmons (1978), successful entrepreneurs have an intense desire to grow and to outperform not just others but to exceed their own previous results. They also keep score; they measure their progress. Moreover, they are not constrained by resources. They believe it's better to have a great idea and no money than a fortune and no idea.

That many entrepreneurs succeed is proven in that we currently have more new businesses in America than at any time in our history, giving rise to a remarkable and prolonged surge in wealth and job creation. In foreign countries, where economies have stagnated in recent years, this phenomenon is called "the American miracle."

ENTREPRENEURSHIP'S IMPACT

Some thought-provoking results have come from this. Consider the following:

- Since 1950, almost all radical innovations in this country have come from infant firms. Examples include the microcomputer, express mailings, and telecommunications.
- From 1980 to 1989, 17 million new jobs were created by predominantly young and smaller firms.
- Entrepreneurs have generated $60 billion of informal risk capital.
- Two million Americans are now classified as millionaires.
- Satisfaction outranks salary as the chief job reward for entrepreneurs.

And now consider this:

- Only 25 percent of the working public professes to be "extremely satisfied" with their jobs. In searching for alternatives, entrepreneurship is listed as an increasingly preferred option.
- Women are starting businesses at a rate nearly two times that of men, and more and more people in their 50s and 60s are starting businesses instead of accepting retirement.

In thinking about entrepreneurship, what does all this mean? Many people start new businesses or try new approaches to existing business but fail, even when they follow all the rules. How do those entrepreneurs who succeed differ from those who don't?

WHAT IS SUCCESS?

Successful entrepreneurs must have three qualities: vision, mission, and passion. They must also understand the nature of true success. Here's what several highly regarded African-American entrepreneurs have to say about success:

Percy Sutton points out that "Success is akin to happiness. Most people search all their lives for success but never find it. Why? Because it lies within."

Terrie Williams, founder of the New York-based public relations agency that bears her name, views success in the same light. "Success has an inner dimension involving spiritual growth, inner peace, and emotional stability," she says. "It goes beyond the dollar sign to encompass inner harmony, comfort, and emotional well-being. I deal with many people who are considered successful, but in most cases, I wouldn't be so quick to agree. While chasing the brass ring, they have allowed joy and happiness to slip through their fingers."

Joshua Smith, founder and CEO of the Maxima Corporation, thinks of success as lying somewhere between personal development and economic freedom. According to Smith, "While it is our responsibility to develop ourselves to the fullest, those whom we would call successful are many times the individuals who've experienced the greatest growth in their lives."

Another Smith, George Smith, founder of Smith Pipe & Supply, offers a variation on this theme: "Some of the most successful people I know— and the happiest, I might add—are those who are doing something they know to be important or personally pleasing, rather than just making a lot of money. This is a key component of success: Doing something you enjoy."

When asked her formula for success, Ernesta Procope, CEO of E.G. Bowman, the only black-owned insurance brokerage firm on Wall Street, replied, "Continuous hard work. Vision. Stubborn determination. Faith. Success rarely deviates or varies its requirements."

Herman Russell, founder of the nation's largest black contractor, says, "Success comes not from doing the impossible, but by doing the possible everyday. It's a long, slow grind."

YOU'D BETTER BE ON A MISSION

Entrepreneurs understand that success and having a mission are often intertwined. Consider the following thoughts and comments:

"The mission of life is success," according to fight promoter Don King. "If you have a talent and don't use it, then you have contributed to your own demise."

And who succeeds? Anyone who takes charge of his or her life.

Alicia Paige, a 50-year-old African-American woman who created Computer Engineering Associates, one of Massachusetts' most profitable high-tech firms, says, "Success means courage." She further suggests that women are frequently called "strong" whenever they overcome adversity but that "courageous" is a better term. Paige says that it took courage to end a lengthy marriage, walk away from a career, and face rejection day-in and day-out. Yet, her advice is that if you want to be successful, you'd better be courageous and on a mission.

Another entrepreneur, Ed Gardner, founder of Soft Sheen Products, a $92 million Chicago-based haircare firm, found the courage to shape his own destiny. "One of my measures for success is what you do for others—your community, the institutions you admire, your fellow man—not just for yourself," he says. "Success means being so good at what you do that your cup runneth over and others benefit."

Amway Product's diamond distributor George Halsey says success is a decision. "Most people never decide to succeed," he says. "They blindly take jobs, and, initially, are ecstatic with their paychecks and prospects. They sell out for security, never considering what that job may cost them in the long run in terms of their own personal development and growth, missed opportunities, and future financial rewards. Success means more than earning a living, it means earning a life."

"It also means paying a price," says A.G. Gaston, a Birmingham, Alabama, business person who picked cotton for pennies a day as a child in Alabama and today operates a series of successful financial and insurance businesses. "If you don't get what you want in life, it's a sign that you either didn't want it bad enough or you tried to haggle over the price."

"Success is a habit," adds chocolate chip cookie mogul Wally Amos. "Unfortunately, so is failing. Each of us is given a blank check and free choice to carve out a successful existence by developing our habits. To do this you start every day with thoughts of 'why not' rather than 'I can't.' Success is the direct result of one's thinking."

Sausage marketer Henry Parks cuts to the heart of the issue. "Once you begin the process of establishing a vision and pursuing that dream with all diligence, you've already succeeded," he says. "This might be one of the best kept secrets regarding success."

WHAT SUCCESS IS AND IS NOT

According to these and other entrepreneurial giants, here is what success is and is not:

Success Is
- An attitude and a matter of choice. It is available to all who will take charge of the direction of their lives. The path to success is led by a sense of mission.

- Success is the process of learning and growing. It requires that the individual be bold enough to hold to a lasting vision and, if necessary, march to the beat of a different drummer. As Essence magazine co-founder Clarence Smith suggested, "Success is not what you have, but what you look forward to."

- Success means sharing your gifts with others; giving, caring, and shaping the lives of others. Many agree the journey should be just as rewarding as the goal attained.

- Succeeding means risk taking, courage, faith, and commitment. Success is born of struggle.

- Success demands the utilization of whatever abilities and talents are available. Entrepreneurs who do what they truly enjoy are the most successful.

Success Is Not
- A destination. Those surveyed never make the assumption that they have arrived. Each keeps driving forward.

- Based only on education. Knowledge is also important. A formal education develops the mind, but success is not what one knows; rather, it is what one does with what one knows.

- Reliant on genius. Successful entrepreneurs place greater importance on personal qualities, such as the ability to concentrate on a single goal for extended periods of time and the ability to exercise good, practical judgments in everyday affairs, rather than on raw intelligence.

- Something that one individual or group can confer upon others.
- A matter of luck. While luck may factor into it, there is no substitute for hard work, long hours, and the ability to get things done.
- A secret. It's simply the implementation of the obvious.

If an entrepreneur has this sense of success, he or she is on the right path. The next ingredient is:

HAVING A VISION

A vision is a target that beckons. Visions animate, inspire, grab, and transform purpose into action.

Historians tend to write about entrepreneurs as if they possess transcendent genius, as if they were capable of creating their missions and sense of destiny out of some mysterious inner resource. But no one is born with a head full of ideas or a proscribed sense of purpose. Instead, successful entrepreneurs seem to have the ability to pick up signals that others miss. They see a pattern that spells opportunity or impending danger. They strive to develop a clear, focused vision in those areas that interest them the most.

When Peter Bynoe set a goal to purchase a professional basketball team or when Percy Sutton sought to acquire a string of radio stations, they were focusing on worthwhile and attainable objectives. "I always keep my creative forces at work by keeping my eyes open," Sutton stated.

Bynoe, one-time co-owner of the Denver Nuggets basketball team, said, "Everything I achieved began with an idea. The secret of my success involves being able to distinguish good ideas from bad ones."

Johnny Ford, mayor of Tuskegee, Alabama, tells this story about Earl G. Graves, editor and publisher of *Black Enterprise* magazine. In 1968, the two men were riding down a busy Manhattan street when Graves pointed at the city's skyscrapers. "See those buildings up there?" he said. "That's where I'm going. By the time I'm 40, I'll be a millionaire. Are you going with me?" Not surprisingly, he achieved this goal.

Successful entrepreneurs learn that nothing can enslave an idea or the imagination. Psychologist Charles Garfield suggests that ideas are the tools needed in constructing a powerful mission, and that great accomplishments are the result of the imagination translated through words and action plans.

A person's full potential emerges not just by developing skills, but by first unlocking the door to the internal resources of the mind that are waiting to be tapped. To unlock that door one must envision a mission—and maintain a dream.

Albert Einstein believed that imagination is more important than knowledge. Einstein claimed that he had only two original ideas during his entire life and that these were the products of his reasoning plus intuition. A human acts, feels, and performs in accordance with what he imagines to be true about himself and his environment. This is the fundamental law of the mind.

PASSION: THE THIRD INGREDIENT

Along with mission and vision, the entrepreneur must have passion. Entrepreneurs are often described as being driven by an intense commitment and determined perseverance. They burn with the competitive desire to excel and win.

In other words, they are filled with passion. The use of this passion in work contributes to success.

Passion can best be translated into action when that action is directed toward something the entrepreneur is committed to and focused on. Most entrepreneurs advise that if the passion is not there, find something else to do.

William Kennedy III was once an office boy to the founder of North Carolina Mutual Insurance Co. Today, Kennedy is president of that firm. In an industry choked with competition for ever-shrinking markets, his solution has been to develop a host of new financial service products that are responsive to consumer needs. Though dwarfed by industry leaders, NCM is highly successful. Why? Because Kennedy knows the formula for success: "People, products, and passion. . . . You'll find all three at NCM."

Finally, when Reg Lewis consummated the deal of the 1980s by acquiring Beatrice Holdings through a 90-to-1 return on McCall's Patterns, he stated: "The sky is the limit. If you believe that you are capable of achieving something and you're willing and disciplined to work at it, then nothing can stop you."

IT TAKES ALL THREE: MISSION, VISION, AND PASSION

What stimulates and sustains this transformation within the entrepreneur, this strong sense of desire and the movement toward achievement, is not insight or education. It's a belief, a Promethean urge, and a passionate desire to step beyond the limits.

AND IT TAKES SOMETHING MORE

What kind of person becomes a successful entrepreneur? What other characteristics does he or she possess?

- **Desire for Independence:** An urge to be your own boss, free from external direction and control. Successful entrepreneurs are self-starters, driven internally to compete and excel against self-imposed standards.

- **Sense of Purpose:** A feeling of mission that motivates. Successful entrepreneurs eagerly take on challenges and test personal abilities to the fullest. They are able to set clear goals that are challenging and attainable.

- **Tolerance of Uncertainty:** The ability to pursue high risk/high return opportunities for which the outcome is in no way certain.

- **Perseverance:** Steadfast pursuit of aim; strong determination to reach objectives regardless of personal sacrifices. Successful entrepreneurs possess the ability to use failure as a learning experience. They are not overly disappointed, discouraged, or depressed by setbacks or failure; rather, they see opportunities and possibilities when confronted by adversity and obstacles.

- **Self-esteem:** A strong sense of self-worth and belief in one's ideas. Entrepreneurs do not believe the success or failure of a venture is governed by fate, luck, "the system," or other powerful, external forces or persons. They believe that their accomplishments as well as setbacks lie within their own control and influence.

- **Salesmanship:** The ability to convince others of the value of their product or service.

- **Self-discipline:** The ability to develop the habits that are necessary to reach important objectives.

Finally, successful entrepreneurs are ready to just plain work hard. J. Bruce Lewellyn, majority owner and chairman of the Philadelphia Coca-Cola Bottling Company and Queen City Broadcasting, summed up what it takes to be a successful entrepreneur when he said:

> Failure is not an overnight experience, and neither is success. Both occur over time and are rarely perceptible to the untrained eye. There are no short cuts. Success emanates from long, hard years of concentrated effort, going the extra mile, maintaining a sense of mission, and doing what others will rarely do. There's an old saying that's very true: "Hard work doesn't guarantee you anything, but without it you don't stand a chance." You can't leave success to chance. You must act on it with a vengeance and pursue it with a passion.

BIBLIOGRAPHY

Bygrave, W. "The Entrepreneurial Paradigm (I): A Philosophical Look at its Research Methodologies," *Entrepreneurship: Theory and Practice* 14, no. 1 (1989): 7–26.

———. "The Entrepreneurial Paradigm (I): Chaos and Catastrophe Among Quantum Jumps? *Entrepreneurship: Theory and Practice* 14, no. 2 (1989): 7–30.

Cromie, S. "Motivations of Aspiring Male and Female Entrepreneurs," *Journal of Occupational Behavior* 8, no. 3 (1987): 251–261.

Dunkelberg, W. C., and A. C. Cooper. "Entrepreneurial Typologies: An Empirical Study." In *Frontiers of Entrepreneurship Research*, edited by Karl H. Vesper. Wellesley, Mass.: Babson College, 1982.

Gasse, Y. *Entrepreneurial Characteristics and Practices: A Study of the Dynamics of Small Business Organizations and Their Effectiveness in Different Environments.* Sherbrooke, Quebec: Rene Prince, 1977.

Hornaday, J. A., and J. Aboud. "Characteristics of Successful Entrepreneurs," *Personnel Psychology* 24 (1971): 141–153.

Kent, C. A., D. L. Sexton, and K. H. Vesper, eds. *Encyclopedia of Entrepreneurship.* Englewood Cliffs, N.J.: Prentice-Hall, 1982.

McClelland, D. C. *The Achieving Society.* Princeton, N.J.: Van Nostrand, 1961.

Rotter, J. B. "Generalized Expectancies for Internal vs. External Control of Reinforcement," *Psychological Monographs* 80, no. 1 (1966):

Schein, E. H. "The Role of the Founder in Creating Organizational Culture," *Organizational Dynamics* 12, no. 1 (1983): 13–28.

Schumpeter, J. "Change and the Entrepreneur." In *Essays of J. A. Schumpeter*, edited by R. Cole, Reading, Mass.: Addison-Wessley, 1934.

Sutton, F. X. *Achievement Norms and the Motivation of Entrepreneurs in Entrepreneurship and Economic Growth.* Cambridge, Mass.: Social Science Research Council and Harvard University Research Center, 1954.

Timmons, J. A. "Characteristics and Role Demands of Entrepreneurship." *American Journal of Small Business* 3, no. 1 (1978): 5–17.

Weber, M. *The Theory of Social and Economic Organization.* Edited and translated by A. M. Henderson and T. Parsons. New York: Free Press, 1947.

2

Leadership Skills of Entrepreneurs: Resolving the Paradoxes and Enhancing the Practices of Entrepreneurial Growth

John H. Eggers and Raymond W. Smilor

Entrepreneurs upset the status quo, disrupt accepted ways of doing things, and alter traditional patterns of behavior. It is often impossible to predict which venture will succeed because of the dynamic nature of the entrepreneurial process.

The critical and essential things that entrepreneurs do include creating and managing change; building effective organizations; serving as resource architects; and marketing and selling in an entrepreneurial fashion. Their leadership skills typically include financial management, communication, motivating others, vision/direction/focus, and motivating self. Skills with a direct bottom-line impact on sales include a clear and committed vision for the organization, the ability to motivate others, and financial and quantitative skills.

A key skill is the entrepreneur's ability to be extremely directive and persuasive yet able to delegate and let go of responsibility. Excellent verbal and listening skills are also very important.

Entrepreneurship is both creative and chaotic. At its most innovative, it is subversive, for entrepreneurs can upset the status quo, disrupt accepted ways of doing things, and alter traditional patterns of behavior. They demonstrate an uncanny knack for recognizing market opportunities and then organizing companies to take advantage of them. As a result, they spur the development of new products and launch new industries (Smilor and Feeser 1991; Stevenson and Harmeling 1990).

Joseph Schumpeter, the Austrian economist who first focused on the role of entrepreneurs in generating innovation for economic well-being, provided an apt, paradoxical description of the process through his concept of "creative destruction," in which new firms tend to impact on the growth, success, and/or failure of existing firms (Schumpeter 1934).

Because of the dynamic nature of the entrepreneurial process, it is often impossible to predict whether a new venture will succeed. Private investors and venture capitalists looking for entrepreneurial investments are often baffled by trying to pick winners. The same is true of government policymakers interested in promoting economic development; business professionals who become involved with new and growing enterprises, hoping they will become paying clients; and corporate managers who support spinoff companies in an attempt to reach new market niches.

So how do we account for success and failure in entrepreneurship? Is the process totally chaotic or are there recognizable patterns in how a company starts and grows? Is the success of a venture really a roll of the dice? Or are there factors within the entrepreneur—factors that can be identified and developed—that directly contribute to increasing the chance of success for the venture?

THE CONTINUUM OF ENTREPRENEURIAL DEVELOPMENT

To think of entrepreneurship as a continuum is to see it as a coherent, and, therefore, understandable and learnable process, sequence, or progression of transition points, critical events, and stages. The more entrepreneurs know about this entrepreneurial continuum and their place on it, the more easily they can recognize patterns and anticipate developments in the entrepreneurial experience, and advance along the continuum. Viewing entrepreneurship this way makes it clear that movement can be backward as well as forward, sometimes skipping a stage of growth, and sometimes encountering ebb and flow. Every stage has different problems and issues—"knotholes"—that may require different learning, different experience, and sometimes different skills (Timmons 1990).

As indicated in Figure 2.1, in the early development stages of a firm (conception and survival), entrepreneurs must address a variety of rather mundane issues. They develop a business plan and perform many diverse tasks as needed to keep the company going. In the stabilization, growth, and rapid-growth stages, entrepreneurs deal with such issues such as hiring, delegating, and structuring for growth. In the mature and decline/regeneration stages, entrepreneurs who have survived and are still in business must figure out how to become entrepreneurial and flexible again.

The key for entrepreneurs is not whether there are different issues and challenges at each of these stages; rather, it is understanding which skills are important across all stages and which may be unique to each, so they can develop and/or enhance those skills that most contribute to movement through the continuum—which ultimately affects the ongoing success of the venture.

Often, the greatest challenge for the entrepreneur is not shifting from an entrepreneurial to a more managerial style as a company grows, but rather is maintaining the entrepreneurial spirit and style while leading a growing and increasingly complex organization.

PARADOXES FACING THE ENTREPRENEUR

A paradox is a set of contradictory or diametrically opposed elements, both of which are real and true, and both of which exist side by side in the same environment at the same time. Perhaps the most compelling aspect of the entrepreneurial process is its paradoxical nature. Only by recognizing the range of paradoxes that exists for entrepreneurs and their ventures is it possible to appreciate the dynamism and unpredictability of the entrepreneurial process as well as the tremendous energy required to move a venture along the entrepreneurial continuum. Managing these paradoxes in a growth venture is the unique responsibility of the entrepreneur.

In the entrepreneurial organization (see Fig. 2.2), order exists side by side with chaos. The very purpose of structure is to try to bring order out

FIGURE 2.1

Continuum of Entrepreneurial Development

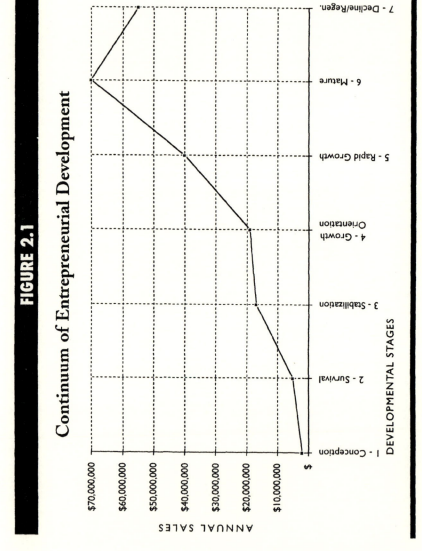

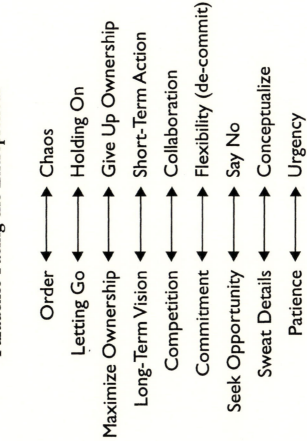

FIGURE 2.2

Paradoxes Facing the Entrepreneur

Order ⟷ Chaos

Letting Go ⟷ Holding On

Maximize Ownership ⟷ Give Up Ownership

Long-Term Vision ⟷ Short-Term Action

Competition ⟷ Collaboration

Commitment ⟷ Flexibility (de-commit)

Seek Opportunity ⟷ Say No

Sweat Details ⟷ Conceptualize

Patience ⟷ Urgency

of chaos as a company grows. Yet, too much order kills the energy and creativity of the building process. The entrepreneur must find a way to hold on to the spirit, purpose, and direction of the company while simultaneously letting go through delegating, allocating responsibility, and letting others make their own mistakes. By giving up ownership in the company through stock options, equity sharing, and incentive plans, the entrepreneur actually maximizes his or her ownership. The entrepreneur must take short-term actions while maintaining long-term vision. This may require that the company collaborate with others, even competitors, through strategic alliances in order to be competitive in the marketplace.

Thus, entrepreneurs commit quickly to a course of action and then decommit or "pull the plug" on that course of action if it proves ineffective. In other words, they seek opportunity but must know when to say no. Entrepreneurs must sweat the details, focusing on each activity day by day while conceptualizing and keeping the big picture in front of them. They must be patient, practicing urgency while striking the precarious balance between getting things done now and waiting for the right time and circumstances to act.

How does one resolve these paradoxes? What skills help the entrepreneur deal with these competing and conflicting requirements?

WHAT ENTREPRENEURS DO

If we ask, "What is it that entrepreneurs do?" we begin to get a sense of their activities and the kinds of skills they must have in order to be successful. Figure 2.3 provides a graphical description of what entrepreneurs do. The following subtopics provide additional details of these activities.

ENTREPRENEURS CREATE AND MANAGE CHANGE

First, entrepreneurs create and manage change. This action-orientation is the essence of what entrepreneurship is all about. By innovating, entrepreneurs continually demonstrate the ability to seize opportunity. Innovation is the means by which entrepreneurs create new wealth-producing resources and utilize existing resources to create additional

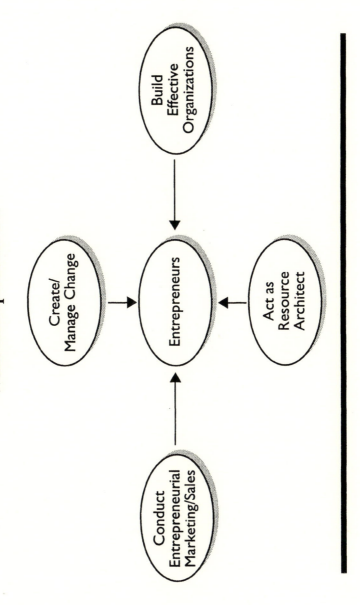

FIGURE 2.3

What Entrepreneurs Do

Build Effective Organizations

Create/Manage Change

Entrepreneurs

Act as Resource Architect

Conduct Entrepreneurial Marketing/Sales

wealth. By converting opportunities into marketable ideas, entrepreneurs become catalysts for change.

Entrepreneurs are often referred to as risk takers, but this isn't quite accurate if we're referring to the gambler who is willing to bet everything on one roll of the dice. A better analogy would be the chess player who may make a bold move yet understands the parameters of the game and anticipates the possible counter moves. Entrepreneurs try to improve their odds by acquiring superior knowledge about the risks. This helps them see the logic rather than the "guts" of an innovation. They are willing to take calculated risks because they have come to terms with the possible ramifications of the innovation. They feel comfortable with the ambiguity and uncertainty—the riskiness—of the changes they are creating.

At the same time, the opportunity to be innovative can never be entirely separated from the opportunity to fail. The person outside of the entrepreneurial process tends to see the "guts" rather than the logic of the innovation. To this person, the entrepreneur can appear to be taking enormous risk and to be making a leap of faith into unknown territory. This is often why business plans are so important to investors, and why venture capitalists always seek to reduce the risk via examining the details of the plan and evaluating the entrepreneur's ability to achieve the results projected in the plan.

ENTREPRENEURS ARE BUILDERS OF EFFECTIVE ORGANIZATIONS

Second, entrepreneurs build effective organizations. As a company grows, successful entrepreneurs get others to buy into the changes they have created, winning not just their involvement but also their commitment to managing that change. This requires clarification of direction and roles from the entrepreneur, along with the development of a reward system for all those who join the enterprise. Consequently, it's critical to the growth of the venture to identify, select, and recruit advisers, board members, and key individuals who will make up the core management team.

It takes vision to build effective organizations. In the entrepreneurial context, vision is the organizational energy that charges behavior, fuels direction, and catalyzes change. It is the unseen but very real fabric of connections that nurture and sustain values.

Entrepreneurial vision can be unconventional. Jack Stack shaped a clear, concise and convincing vision for Springfield Remanufacturing Corporation (SRC) when he took over a company in desperate straits in 1982. Faced with an 89:1 debt-to-equity ratio, a labor versus management mindset, and an environment of uncertainty and doubt, he told the other 119 owners of their new company, "Don't run out of cash and don't destroy from within" (Stack 1992). They never have. This vision built a culture of education, open information about all financials, ownership, teamwork, and performance that gained SRC recognition as one of the 100 best companies to work for in America.

Margaret Wheatley relates the concept of force fields in nature (such as the force of gravity and magnetic fields) to organization leadership. We know that these force fields exist and that they exert powerful influences over objects with which they come in contact. Yet, they are invisible. She says, "I have come to understand organizational vision as a field—a force of unseen connections that influence employees' behavior—rather than as an evocative message about some future state" (Wheatley 1993).

Neal Patterson and Clifford Illig, the visionary leaders of Cerner Corporation, argue that it is better to build "a visionary company rather than a company of visionaries." This may be one reason Cerner has become such a successful company. It is an organization creating its own force field in which each person energizes and is energized by a powerful shared vision.

ENTREPRENEURS ARE RESOURCE ARCHITECTS

Third, entrepreneurs act as resource architects. They demonstrate the ability to maximize every kind of resource. According to Stevenson and Gumpert (1985), entrepreneurship is "the pursuit of opportunity beyond the resources currently controlled." This has powerful implications for the financial management of an entrepreneurial venture. Wanting to keep their options open and knowing resources may be limited, entrepreneurs will search for effectiveness rather than efficiency.

They may also maximize resources through networks. Important research on the sociology of the entrepreneurial process shows that entrepreneurship is enhanced or constrained by the ties, linkages, and associations between entrepreneurs, resources, and opportunities (Aldrich and Zimmer 1986). Consequently, success in entrepreneurial ventures requires linking relationships not only among and between individuals but also among and between a variety of institutions.

Forming a strategic alliance between emerging entrepreneurial companies and larger organizations is a way to extend the resources of the entrepreneur (Botkin and Matthews 1992). The more extensive, complex, and diverse the web of relationships, the more the entrepreneur is likely to have access to the resources of others. This gives the entrepreneur a better chance of solving problems expeditiously and offers a greater chance of success for a growth venture. The less dense and more homogenous the web of relationships, the less likely it is for a growth venture to succeed.

THE ENTREPRENEUR KNOWS THE MARKETPLACE

Fourth, entrepreneurs market and sell in an entrepreneurial fashion. They sense the pulse of the customer and then match real products with real customer needs. As a result, rather than only seeking shares of existing markets, they build relationships, find new users, and develop better and expanded applications for products to generate new market opportunities. They constantly seek innovative, even experimental, ways to watch, evaluate, sense, interact with, respond to, and anticipate customers. In this way, entrepreneurs not only are learning from the marketplace but also are constantly educating it. The learning and teaching are inseparable, continually reinforcing and expanding the other (Smilor 1989).

When a product solves a real problem or meets a real need, it reflects a deep understanding of the customer. When the customer is educated to the product's values and benefits, the result can be the "ah ha" sensation of discovery that comes with customer-driven products. To educate oneself about the marketplace, the entrepreneur must have quantitative information and qualitative insights. One springs from data, the other from experience. One relies on numbers, the other on judgment. One demands objectivity, the other personal involvement.

This allows entrepreneurs to actually create markets for new products and services by experimenting with product designs, developing innovative approaches to servicing customers, and utilizing intangibles to gain a share of mind and not just a share of market.

CREATING A MAJOR STUDY OF ENTREPRENEURIAL LEADERSHIP SKILLS

If these are the critical and essential things that entrepreneurs do, then what skills help them do these things better?

The balance of this chapter describes the results of a study by the authors conducted in an effort to understand what skills are most helpful to the entrepreneurs as they confront and resolve paradoxes in the management of growth in their firms.

DESIGNING THE RESEARCH STUDY

The study sampled firms from four different databases to replicate the natural small business population for geography, ethnicity, gender, and industry. Respondents were drawn from the Ernst & Young Entrepreneur of the Year Institute®, the Executive Committee (TEC), Connecticut Mutual's Blue Chip Enterprise Initiative, and the Small Business Administration PASS Database in Washington, D.C.

A combination of qualitative and quantitative methods were utilized to answer the questions previously raised. This approach, often referred to as a multimethod/multitrait design (Campbell and Fisk 1959) is time-consuming but is more accurate and less biased than simpler, less complex approaches to obtaining information.

THE QUALITATIVE SURVEY

The Entrepreneurial Leadership Questionnaire (ELQ) (Eggers and Leahy 1992) was mailed to 2,608 people from the four groups previously mentioned. Three hundred thirty-eight completed surveys were returned for a response rate of 13 percent. The ELQ utilizes an open response format designed to identify leadership and management skills used by the respondents. An advantage of this approach is its potential for generating and reflecting the subjects' full thoughts on the subject matter (Conrad and Maul 1981).

The questionnaire asked the participants to list the leadership and management skills they needed to successfully run their businesses and indicate their relative level of importance. A five-point Likert scale was used to indicate level of importance.

Participants were asked to define the stage of development of the firm according to the model developed by Churchill and Lewis (1983); to identify the stage they wished to achieve; and to determine if the leadership skills at the next level or stage of growth would be different from those used currently. If different skills were expected, the respondents were asked to identify them.

Participants were also asked to identify the previous developmental stage of their businesses and to identify and rank the leadership and management skills needed to run their businesses at that stage. This process continued until participants had identified all previous stages of business development and all critical skills for each previous stage. They were then asked to respond to questions related to the accuracy of the model in defining the growth of the business and identify any stages of growth that did not apply to their firms.

Thus, the study identified three perspectives of leadership and management skills based on current, previous, and desired state of development.

Additional demographic and performance data were also collected. The characteristics and gender of the respondents are shown in Table 2.1. The company demographics are shown in Table 2.2.

THE QUANTITATIVE SURVEY

The Management Skills Profile (MSP) (Personnel Decisions Inc. 1982) was administered to the 346 respondents to the ELQ questionnaire approximately three weeks after receipt of the survey. Two hundred and twenty-one useable responses were returned for a response rate of 67 percent. The respondents were normally distributed across the stages of business development (Fig. 2.4). The MSP measures 18 skills and one research scale. These skills, as defined by Van Velsor and Leslie (1991), are presented in Table 2.3.

KEY FINDING: SKILLS ACROSS STAGES

The analysis of the ELQ revealed 9,690 responses falling into 34 content areas. Statements were ranked in order of importance using a total weight score for each item based on the Likert score for each statement (ranging from 1 to 5) multiplied by the total number of statements.

The top five skills identified across all stages of development were: 1) financial management, 2) communication, 3) motivating others, 4) vision/

TABLE 2.1

CEO Characteristics and Gender

Survey Response	Female, N = 68			Male, N = 269			Group Total	
	Mean	Mode	Count	Mean	Mode	Count	Mean	Mode
Age	45 yrs.	46 yrs.	2 & 5	48 yrs.	50 yrs.	19 & 20	48 yrs.	50 yrs.
Current Development Stage	Growth Orient.	Growth Orient.	27	Growth Orient.	Growth Orient.	103	Growth Orient.	Growth Orient.
No. of Direct Reports	6	4	4 & 7	7	5	18 & 25	7	5
Desired Development Stage	Rapid Growth	Mature	14 & 29	Rapid Growth	Mature	47 & 122	Rapid Growth	Mature
Years in Industry	16 yrs.	20 yrs.	3 & 9	20 yrs.	20 yrs.	41	19 yrs.	20 yrs.
Percentage of Ownership	64%	100%	2 & 22	58%	100%	1 & 73	59%	100%

TABLE 2.2

Company Demographics

Characteristic	Combined Sample, N = 338		
	Mean	Median	Mode
Business Age	24 yrs.	15 yrs.	10 yrs.
Current Development Stage	4	4	4
Number of Locations	7	2	1
Business Area Covered	National	National	Global
Current Annual Sales	$27,291,543	$9,805,000	$5,000,000
Average Annual Sales Increase	$1,922,315	$800,000	$1,000,000
First Year Sales	$1,056,383	$150,000	$100,000
Total Employees	223	73	30
Total Full-time Employees	141	60	30

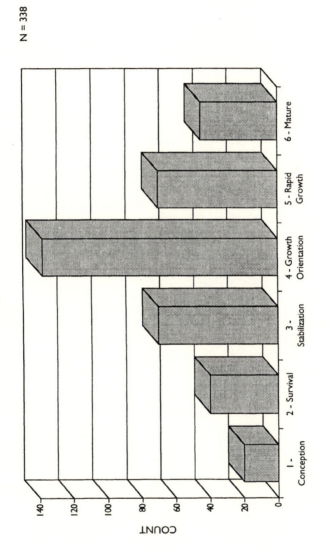

FIGURE 2.4

Current Stages of Development

N = 338

29

TABLE 2.3

MSP Scales

1. Planning

2. Organizing

3. Personal Organization and Time Management

4. Informing

5. Oral Communication

6. Listening

7. Written Communication

8. Problem Analysis and Decision Making

9. Financial and Quantitative

10. Human Relations

11. Conflict Management

12. Leadership Style and Influence

13. Motivating Others

14. Delegating and Controlling

15. Coaching and Developing

16. Personal Motivation

17. Personal Adaptability

18. Occupational/Technical Knowledge

19. Results Orientation

direction/focus, and 5) motivating self. (See Table 2.4 for a complete listing of responses.)

A number of interconnected themes appeared within each content dimension. The themes for the top five categories emerged as follows:

TABLE 2.4

ELQ Content Analysis Dimensions Across Developmental Stages

Content Area	Total Weight	Number of Statements	Scale Mean
1. Financial Management	3,817	900	4.24
2. Communication*	2,752	653	4.21
3. Motivating Others	2,517	615	4.09
4. Vision	2,353	522	4.51
5. Motivating Self	2,239	496	4.51
6. Planning/Goal Setting	2,096	488	4.30
7. Marketing	1,787	414	4.32
8. Relationship Building	1,736	425	4.08
9. Human Resources	1,731	417	4.15
10. Problem Solving/Decision Making	1,701	395	4.31
11. Business/Technical Knowledge	1,516	384	3.95
12. Sales	1,506	335	4.50
13. Leadership/Management	1,453	334	4.35
14. Employee Development	1,423	340	4.19
15. Customer/Vendor Relations	1,274	289	4.41
16. Ethics/Organizational Culture	1,267	272	4.66
17. Organizing	1,236	311	3.97
18. Delegating	1,205	297	4.06
19. Personal Adaptability	1,170	290	4.03
20. Time Management	1,126	299	3.77
21. Product/Business Development	886	204	4.34
22. Systems Development	864	222	3.89
23. Quality Control	826	201	4.11
24. Creativity/Innovation	476	116	4.10
25. Listening	473	111	4.26
26. Results Orientation	414	100	4.14
27. Risk Taking	389	87	4.47
28. Negotiation/Conflict Resolution	385	93	4.14
29. Informing	374	92	4.07
30. Oral Communication	225	59	3.81
31. Self-Development	213	49	4.35
32. Administration	191	56	3.41
33. Miscellaneous	177	43	4.12
34. Written Communication	137	33	4.15

*Category includes: Informing, Listening, Oral Communication and Written Communication.

Financial Management

The content of this area revolved around two challenges that emerging businesses face.

The first is acquiring and maintaining adequate capital for the business. Three activities were reported as critical to performing this successfully: 1) finding appropriate sources of funding, 2) securing funding from identified sources, and 3) maintaining good relations with the funding source to ensure long-term availability of funding. The two primary sources of funding were identified as commercial banks and independent investors (often referred to as "angels").

The second challenge is using the acquired funds wisely, a challenge seen as being accomplished through the application of accounting skills and general accounting knowledge. Successful entrepreneurs defined wise use of capital as maintaining adequate cash reserves by anticipating cash needs, controlling spending, collecting receivables, and monitoring cash flow.

Communication

The two dimensions reported as critical to communication were inter- and intrapersonal communication. Entrepreneurs in the study identified the ability to express even complex ideas in a clear, simple, and direct manner as the foundation for all successful communication. Application of these skills applies not only to one-on-one communications but also to large group presentations.

However, the ability to communicate ideas outwardly was only a portion of how they defined successful communication. Of equal importance was the willingness to listen to others in a sincere and open manner, using active listening skills to show speakers they are being heard and that their ideas are being valued and respected. This willingness to be open to other views extends beyond interpersonal communications to the larger picture of creating an organization that values this as a cultural norm.

Entrepreneurs also focused on the content of communication. They indicated that communicating the company's vision, goals, and plans in a way that inspires understanding and action was critical. The receivers of this communication are not only the organization's employees but also its customers and vendors.

Motivating Others

The respondents reported that they achieve their vision by motivating others. They accomplish this by developing their employees into highly motivated teams that understand and support the vision of the organization and have a sense of urgency in making it a reality. Further, they create and inspire the loyalty and trust of their employees and reward team effort while acknowledging individual contributions.

Vision/Direction/Focus

Entrepreneurs defined "vision" as the ability to create and communicate a clear direction for the company's future, often seeing opportunities long before others do. Along with this ability to see the "big picture," they also develop the skill and commitment to stay focused on achieving their vision. They report that it is critical not to become sidetracked or deterred by the inevitable problems that occur along the way.

Motivating Self

Entrepreneurial leaders report that the difference between those who achieve their vision and those who do not is the ability to "stay up" in the process and give 110 percent effort, day in and day out. They report that this takes the form of a passionate commitment to action, combined with a fiercely competitive attitude of "can do." This effort requires energy, self-discipline, resilience, and an extremely strong work ethic.

KEY FINDINGS: SKILLS AND COMPANY PERFORMANCE

Analysis of the results of the MSP and the ELP identified three skills with a direct impact on the sales of the organization.

These skills are: 1) a clear and committed vision for the organization; 2) the ability of the entrepreneur to motivate others; and 3) the financial and quantitative skills of the entrepreneur.

The entrepreneurs' skill levels in these three areas contributed to 17 percent of the current sales of their companies. The higher the skill level, the higher the current sales of their organizations.

What do highly successful entrepreneurs do to create a vision, motivate others to follow and work toward that vision, and stay in business during the process? The study offers insight.

The key is the ability of the entrepreneur to appropriately "flex" the way he or she leads. This involves using a complex but clear matrix of skills, which on the surface may appear contradictory and paradoxical. Highly successful entrepreneurial leaders are able to be extremely directive and persuasive, yet are able to delegate and let go of responsibility. This allows employees to develop their own skills and abilities through experience, even if some of that experience results in failure rather than success. This approach works for these entrepreneurs because of the respect they command from others and the trust they instill in their employees and their organizations.

These same entrepreneurs have excellent verbal skills, which are critical to selling and communicating the vision they have for the future. Yet they are also highly developed listeners. They are able to create cultures within their organizations that value action and the achievement of their vision. And when they obtain the vision, they share the rewards.

KEY FINDINGS: NONLINEAR GROWTH

An examination of the developmental patterns of organizations in the study revealed that only 51 percent of the companies progressed sequentially, following a traditional linear pattern of development and growth. Hence, 49 percent developed in a nonlinear progression. In addition, 34 percent of the firms skipped traditional stages of development (See Fig. 2.5).

Of the organizations that skipped developmental stages, not all experienced increased growth for long. Eight percent of the companies in the study dropped back in development, regressing to an earlier stage after their leap forward. Another seven percent simply regressed to an earlier stage instead of maintaining a forward progression. Some differences in skill levels were revealed between those firms that skipped stages forward and those that regressed a stage in development. The MSP scores on leadership, personal motivation, organizing, and time management were significantly higher for those firms that skipped forward than for those that regressed in stages of development (see Table 2.5).

FIGURE 2.5

The Development Dynamics of Emerging High Growth Companies

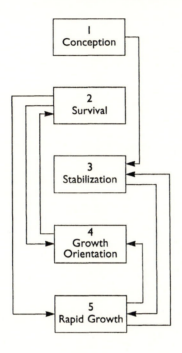

Linear vs. Nonlinear Growth

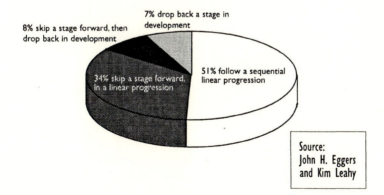

8% skip a stage forward, then drop back in development

7% drop back a stage in development

34% skip a stage forward, in a linear progression

51% follow a sequential linear progression

Source:
John H. Eggers
and Kim Leahy

TABLE 2.5

Linear Versus Nonlinear Growth

Organizations that drop back a stage in their development (nonlinear) have entrepreneurs reporting lower levels of management/leadership skills as compared to organizations that grow sequentially.

Skill	Accelerated Linear Growth Skipping a Stage Forward	Traditional Sequential Linear Growth	Nonlinear, Dropping Back a Development Stage	Nonlinear, Skipping a Stage Forward, then Dropping Back
	Mean	Mean	Mean	Mean
Leadership	Highest**	Higher**	Lowest**	Lower**
Personal Motivation	High*	High*	Lowest*	n.s.
Organizing	Higher*	Higher*	Lowest*	n.s.
Time Management	Higher**	Highest**	Lowest**	Low**

*p<.05
**p<.01

SUMMARY AND IMPLICATIONS

The results of this study, based on a large scale sample of entrepreneurs' responses to two valid and reliable instruments, have supported many of the established concepts of leadership and growth, questioned some, and showed that others have only limited applicability to emerging firms.

Most of the leadership styles normally attributed to entrepreneurs have been supported. What is interesting to note is that a single leadership style may not be appropriate across all growth stages, rates of growth, or levels of firm complexity. In addition, the ability of growth stage models to explain growth in emerging firms appears to be severely limited.

BIBLIOGRAPHY

Aldrich, Howard, and Catherine Zimmer. "Entrepreneurship Through Social Networks." In *The Art and Science of Entrepreneurship,* edited by Donald L. Sexton and Raymond W. Smilor, 3–23. Cambridge, Mass.: Ballinger Publishing Company, 1986.

Botkin, James W., and Jana Matthews. *Winning Combinations.* New York: John Wiley, 1992.

Campbell, D. T., and D. W. Fiske. "Convergent and Discriminate Validation by the Multi-Trait–Multi-Method Matrix," *Psychological Bulletin* 56 (1959): 81–105.

Churchill, N. C., and V. L. Lewis, "The Five Stages of Small Business Growth," *Harvard Business Review* (May/June 1983): 30–50.

Conrad, E., and T. Maul. *Introduction to Experimental Psychology.* New York: John Wiley & Sons, Inc., 1981.

Eggers, J. H., and K. Leahy. *Entrepreneurial Leadership Questionnaire.* San Diego, Cal.: Center for Creative Leadership, 1992.

Personnel Decisions Inc. *Management Skills Profile (MSP).* Minneapolis, Minn.: PDI, 1982.

Schumpeter, J. A. *The Theory of Economic Development.* Cambridge, Mass.: Harvard University Press, 1934.

Stack, Jack. *The Great Game of Business.* New York: Currency Books, 1992.

Smilor, Raymond W., *Customer-Driven Marketing: Lessons from Entrepreneurial Technology Companies.* Cambridge, Mass.: Lexington Books, 1989.

Smilor, Raymond W., and Henry Feeser. "Chaos and the Entrepreneurial Process, Patterns and Policy Implications for Technology Entrepreneurship," *Journal of Business Venturing* 6, no. 3 (1991): 165–72.

Stevenson, Howard, and David Gumpert. "The Heart of Entrepreneurship," *Harvard Business Review* 63, no. 2 (1985): 85–94.

Stevenson, Howard, and Susan Harmeling. "Entrepreneurial Management's Need for a More 'Chaotic' Theory," *Journal of Business Venturing* 5, no. 1 (1990): 1–14.

Timmons, Jeffry A. *New Venture Creation: Entrepreneurship in the 1990s,* 3rd ed. Boston: Irwin, 1990.

Van Velsor, E., and J. B. Leslie. *Feedback to Managers Volume II: A Review and Comparison of Sixteen Multi-Rate Feedback Instruments.* Greensboro, N.C.: Center for Creative Leadership, 1991.

Wheatley, Margaret. *Leadership and the New Science.* San Francisco: Barett-Kohler Publishing Co., 1993.

3

Creating the Uncommon Company
Ewing M. Kauffman

Two key principles have guided my success in business: 1) those who produce should share in the profits, and 2) treat others as you would be treated.

If associates are allowed to share in the profits, they will work hard to make money for you. This can be achieved by setting yearly goals and by telling your people how much their bonus can be if the goals are achieved. Stock option programs are important. They allow associates to feel a real sense of company ownership. Treat others as you would be treated is based on the realization that people will live up to or down to your expectations. Treating people well is the happiest and most intelligent principle there is for making money.

Hiring the right people is also important. When hiring executives, look for intelligence, experience, capability, and a genuine caring about people.

Managers should be called "leaders." People don't want to be managed, but they like to be led. Managers should be fair, honest, and truthful. The best company has an environment where people like to be and has people who want to work.

> Do not choose to be a common company. Take a calculated
> risk: to dream, to build, and to succeed. By sharing your prof-
> its and treating others as you would be treated, you will be
> successful and you will also be happy.

As a pharmaceutical salesman, I learned some important lessons about how *not* to run an organization and these helped me formulate the principles I utilized in starting and building Marion Laboratories, which is now Marion Merrell Dow. Here's how that came about:

In 1947, I saw an advertisement in the paper for a pharmaceutical salesman position. I knew nothing about pharmaceuticals, but I was intrigued because the company said applicants must take an aptitude test. I always did enjoy taking tests, so I applied for the job and got it.

I fell in love with the business. I read and studied about it all the time. I worked on straight commission, receiving no salary, no expenses, no car, and no benefits in any way, shape, or form—just straight commission.

By the end of the second year, my commission amounted to more than the president's salary. He didn't think that was right, so he cut my commission. By then I was Midwest sales manager and had other salesmen working for me under an arrangement whereby my commission was three percent of everything they sold. In spite of the cut in my commission, that year I still managed to make more than the president thought a sales manager should make. So this time he cut the territory, which was the same as taking away some of my income. I quit and started Marion Laboratories.

That was in 1950. I started the business with an investment of $5,000 and three good clients. My task was selling pharmaceuticals by day and packaging tablets in my basement at night. Marion Labs had a sales force of one: myself. The first year, sales were $36,000. When Marion Laboratories merged with Merrell Dow in 1989, the company was valued at $6 billion.

I based the company on a vision of what it would be. When we hired employees, they were referred to as "associates," and they shared in the success of the company. Once again, the two principles that have guided my entire career, which were based on my experience working for that very first pharmaceutical company, are these: "Those who produce should share in the profits," and "Treat others as you would be treated."

SHARE THE PROFITS

One did not need to be a mathematical genius to calculate that the more money Marion associates made, the more money the company would make. If the company made a profit, everyone who worked there was entitled to a bonus—not just the top-level executives, but everyone.

People are motivated by setting yearly goals and telling each associate the bonus he or she could earn. Goals can be based on sales if you can accurately forecast expenses; otherwise, goals should be based on profits. Since some associates would do better than others, we devised three levels of performance appraisal: "good" meant they received 85 percent of their bonus; "excellent" meant they received 100 percent of their bonus; and "outstanding" meant they received 120 percent of their bonus.

In those early days, our people were assured that they would soon have medical and disability benefits and that there would be a profit-sharing retirement program as well. Also, I've always believed it's the inherent right of everyone who works at our company to own stock in it. This makes a tremendous difference in how they feel about the organization because they feel a sense of ownership. They actually tell their friends and neighbors, "I own part of my company."

When Marion Laboratories merged with Merrell Dow, senior managers and many plant and clerical workers who had been with the firm for a long time were able to realize significant wealth from their stock in the company. In fact, approximately 300 millionaires were created during the merger.

THE GOLDEN RULE CAN BE A TOUGH SELL

My second principle has always been a tough sell to business people, and not too many businesses have adopted it—though several adopted it and become very successful. "Treat others as you want to be treated" sounds like the Golden Rule, but it doesn't have to be based on religion. It's how we should treat all people, in and out of business.

People have a tendency to live up to or down to your expectations, so the more you expect from them, the more they will accomplish. If you treat your customers the way you would like to be treated as a customer, they will be loyal. If you treat your employees the way you wanted to be treated when you were an employee, they will be happier and more productive. If you treat your suppliers the way you would like to be treated in supplying other companies, you will be amazed at the quality of service you will receive. Treating others the way you would like to be treated is the happiest and most intelligent principle in the world for making money.

HIRING THE RIGHT PEOPLE

Entrepreneurs have to learn that they can't do it all themselves. If you get six other people to help you and you have hired the right people, you'll have multiplied your efforts by at least a factor of five, and maybe more if they are really good.

Here are a few things I've learned about finding the right people. Three qualities to look for, especially when you're hiring at the executive level, are intelligence, experience, and capability. The most important quality, however, is genuinely caring about people. If someone didn't have this quality, they couldn't fit into the culture of Marion Laboratories, where we strictly believed in treating others like we wanted to be treated—not only from above, but at all levels.

Occasionally, mistakes were made in hiring. In one instance, a particular executive couldn't get along with people. He would do things such as tell his associates at 3:30 p.m. that he had scheduled a meeting for 5 p.m.— even when he knew many of them were supposed to get off work at 4:30 p.m. He showed no consideration for whether they had anything to do that night. And then, instead of commencing the meeting at 5 p.m., he might not show up until 5:15. It was clear that he didn't care for people. We brought this to his attention, telling him he had to improve or leave. Four of us worked with him for a year, meeting with him every week to explain the things we wanted him to learn. But he didn't learn and he had to leave.

THE ENTREPRENEUR AS LEADER

When people talk about managers, they are using the wrong word. People don't want to be managed, but they don't mind being led. The word "manager" should be changed to "leader."

It's complex being a leader. Goals for the group allow for individual goals to be met. At the same time, the individual's goals must be in harmony with company objectives. You can tell people anything, but it means nothing unless you put it into action. In other words, action means much more than words. One rule I've lived by as a leader is to always tell the truth, no matter how tough it is or whether it is good news or bad news. Telling the truth gives credibility to you personally and to your company. Your people can trust you. They know you have integrity and that, as their leader, you will do what is right and you will be fair. This means you live what you preach. You do things right—all the time, day after day.

Finally, as a leader, it's your job to build your associates' esteem. The more confident they feel, the better the job they will do. One of the most motivating forces in the world is appreciation. Most of us don't express appreciation to others as much as we should. When people do worthwhile things, tell them how much it means to you and your company.

This brings up the importance of communication, another important component of business success. If you can communicate your business principles and vision, you will gain your associates' support for the company. The more they know, the better they can do their jobs. Communicating means listening to them. You will learn more that way than any other.

CREATING A SUCCESSFUL COMPANY

To create the most successful company possible, an atmosphere must be created in which every employee understands the basic beliefs and purposes that breathe life and meaning into everything involving your company. The difference between mediocrity and excellence in business is in creating an environment in which associates are constantly challenged and in which mediocrity is not accepted. This will be an environment in which people will want to work and produce.

It is my firm belief that most people want to work. There are a few who are lazy, but most do want to work, provided three conditions are met:

1. They are adequately compensated.

2. They are appreciated by management.

3. They believe they are part of the company.

In examining the growth of Marion Labs, it becomes apparent that following these principles is the path to success.

PRINCIPLES IN ACTION

Many people think the pharmaceutical industry has high profits because it sells patented products with high markups. Yet, for 30 years our company had no patented products. Marion Laboratories competed with hundreds of other pharmaceutical companies that were selling identical products. In fact, in the beginning our products were manufactured for us by other companies.

Because of the culture and spirit we created among our associates, we became number one among all 300 pharmaceutical companies in sales per employee and in profits per employee, and it was done without a single patented product.

Within 15 years Marion Labs went public in the over-the-counter market, still with no patented products. By 1980, sales had topped $100 million per year. Profits, after taxes, were $7 million a year—and we still had no patented products. One share of stock sold to the public in 1965 had split to become 192 shares in 1980, and the stock (now listed on the New York Stock Exchange) had a value of $7 billion.

PUTTING IT ALL TOGETHER

What is the difference between a mediocre company, a good one, and an excellent one? The best companies are not those that develop the most charts and graphs or the biggest research facility or the largest methods department or the greatest complexity.

The best company is one in which a favorable environment reflects management philosophies of trust and respect, an absence of restraints that limit individual development, and one that offers individual recognition, opportunity, and fair treatment.

A code of ethics based on your relationship with your associates must be developed. It's the people who become your associates who will make the difference. If you care about people, and they know you care about them, a spirit and a culture will be created that makes them want to come to work in the morning and makes them proud to be associated with the company.

This culture is based on a trust of everyone who works for the firm. There will be occasions when the trust is misplaced, but in the long run you will be ahead both company-wise and profit-wise, and certainly you will be happier.

As an entrepreneur, do not choose to be a common company. It's your right to be uncommon if you can. Seek opportunity to compete. Take the calculated risk: to dream, to build, and to succeed. In following your dream, you may not be as lucky as we were, but if you build your company based on sharing your profits and treating others as you would be treated, you will be successful—and you will also be happier.

4

Pearls of Wisdom from Mr. Kauffman on What Makes Entrepreneurship Work

Neal Patterson

Ewing Kauffman, the founder of Marion Laboratories and a great entrepreneur, shared several pearls of wisdom that have made a difference for Cerner Corporation.

The first involved language, specifically the difference between the words "employee" and "associate." "Employee" connotes hierarchy, and hierarchy doesn't work in a corporation such as Cerner, which is knowledge-based and at which all the knowledge is down below because technology changes so fast.

Mr. K also advised entrepreneurs to have a vision for their business. American scientists put a man on the moon because they could envision it. At Cerner Corporation, the future is envisioned every day and is described to our associates and our clients. To make certain that associates fully understand what's going on in the business and feel that they are an important part of it, everyone gets together periodically—another idea from Mr. K—and talks about the business.

To get public visibility, early in its life Cerner concentrated more on establishing its vision than on making money. Gradually, a presence was established that helped create value.

Cerner has been successful because of a strong belief in its vision and associates. And, following Mr. K's advice, the vision became more powerful because it was effectively communicated. Other gems from Mr. K that have impacted Cerner's success include work hard and have fun.

Ewing Kauffman, the founder of Marion Laboratories, now part of Marion Merrell Dow, was generous in sharing many of his pearls—little nuggets of wisdom he had learned in his years of doing business with others. I was one of the fortunate people with whom he shared his ideas. This chapter explains how they have impacted on Cerner Corporation.

First, a word about Cerner. Our product is software that processes information about patients and their medical problems, providing consistency so that more than one provider can care for a patient. While most people think only in terms of doctors and nurses delivering medical care, in reality, many people are involved. It's a team approach. As health care becomes more and more community-based, information technology is going to be more important than ever in ensuring quality, coordinated care by tracking everything that happens to a patient.

Back to Mr. K. Cerner is an entrepreneurial company, and Mr. K contributed to our success in several ways. For example, Cerner does not have "employees," we have "associates." Mr. K understood the nuances of language and knew the important difference between these two words. Using the term "associates" instead of "employees" is part of the current thinking in building successful organizations. Mr. K developed this approach in the 1970s.

The word "employee" connotes hierarchy. In business, hierarchy may be an impediment to success. Cerner is a knowledge organization that is based on technology. We create software containing knowledge about processes. Last year, our software affected more than 10 million patients. Hierarchy is worthless in an organization such as Cerner because the knowledge by which we operate is with employees traditionally viewed as being at the bottom of the hierarchy. We're not a company where the person above has done the job below and could do it better than the person now doing it. Today, technology is changing so rapidly that all the knowledge rests with the technicians, not the managers. So if the organization is knowledge-based and is built on hierarchy, trouble is just around the corner.

HAVING AND COMMUNICATING A VISION FOR YOUR COMPANY

Mr. K also shared the importance of having a vision of what one's company should look like in the future. Nothing is going to happen unless it first is envisioned.

President Kennedy did this with the space program by setting the goal to be the first country to put a man on the moon. Nothing was said about competition or why it was important that the United States achieve this goal. A vision of greatness was simply presented.

American scientists understood the vision and set out to achieve the objective. This task had never been done before and many technical problems needed to be solved, but corrections were made as needed and the vision remained intact. What they learned is that when you go to the moon, you don't go in a straight line. You go zigzag, zigzag, zigzag. Visions are like that, too. We have a vision at Cerner for the year 2005. This vision is described every day to people starting new projects and to clients. But there are no two areas moving faster in our society than technology and health care, and just like the scientists' vision of going to the moon, our vision changes over time as we learn and solve problems.

Mr. K said that while entrepreneurs create things, they aren't the ones who continue them. To be successful, the entrepreneur must construct an organization with groups of people to run it. People must understand the entrepreneur's vision to have a purpose for their work. This is done at Cerner by making everyone an executive as well as a manager. Managers are the lubricant that makes an organization work. Our people are managers because they focus on the plan and help execute it. But they also are executives because, unlike managers, they are members of the team that looks to the year 2005 and determines how to achieve the vision.

It also is necessary that our public understands the vision. A vision center at Cerner has been built to communicate the vision to our clients. Incidentally, we don't call them customers or vendors. Learning from Mr. K that just as "associate" is a better word than "employee," "client" is also a better word than "customer" or "vendor," which refers to a transaction. The word "client" speaks about a relationship. Our approach is to build a relationship with our clients, who we hope will see us as clients and not as vendors.

Cerner's vision also is communicated through two publications, one for our clients and one for our associates. They are mailed to home addresses so the associates/clients can read them at their leisure and share them with their families. These publications discuss the current state of the firm and the vision for the future. Vision is shared and debate is encouraged.

THE IMPORTANCE OF THE INDIVIDUAL

Town hall meetings are another of Mr. K's ideas that we employ. When growth prevented gathering all the associates in a room at the firm, Mr. K suggested that we bus associates to a location that would allow us to meet together. Now, we meet with more than 600 people in an auditorium. It is essential that associates understand how important they are to the organization. This is accomplished by sharing stories about what we do at work. The importance of Cerner's product to health care and of health care to the nation is such that our associates recognize that their loved ones' lives depend upon it. They also recognize that they, too, will end up in a health care system that has some Cerner software controlling information about their health status.

A Cerner executive was misquoted by the press in saying that our goal at Cerner was to have 1,000 employees. Cerner's goal has never been to grow; rather, it is to realize our vision and to achieve the future we have described for ourselves. We will be larger because health care is going to be larger, but that in itself is not the goal.

MAKING OUR VISION COME TRUE

Early in Cerner's history—when the company was young and no one would believe we had a product, let alone a vision—we raised around $3 million for our venture. That's not much money today, but back then it was, especially since we were still losing money. To make a long story short, growth and profitability allowed Cerner to purchase another company, resulting in an additional $80 million for Cerner shareholders.

When we were trying to raise those first funds, one of our advisors told us to concentrate on creating a presence. This was sound advice. Now that we have achieved a presence, it is much easier to attract the attention of *The Wall Street Journal, Fortune,* or *Forbes.* Value is created by working diligently to achieve presence. Sometimes unbelievable sacrifices were made, but we had to make all associates become executives with vision and managers who made it happen. This was achievable because all involved knew that a future was being created.

Cerner could have been a highly profitable laboratory systems company. Instead, in order to make the vision a reality, most of the profits were reinvested in the firm. For several years we spent money as fast as we made it. Wall Street wasn't pleased because they were concerned about the next quarter's results. But we were dedicated to fulfilling our vision. We had described a future in which we believed.

Everyone in the company believed in the vision and still does. A recent survey showed that more than 90 percent of the associates at Cerner said they understood and believed in our vision. The results are phenomenal when you realize that 10 percent of those people were hired fewer than six months prior to the survey. Wall Street did not understand the vision, and the price of Cerner stock dropped for a period of time. In today's terms, it was under $2.00 at one point. More recently it was over $40.00.

Why has Cerner been successful? In part, because we have believed in our own strength and in what we can do, and because we had the right idea at the right time. A vision is essential in order to take advantage of opportunities. Thanks to those pearls of wisdom from Mr. K, we determined a vision for Cerner, communicated it to our associates and clients, and made the effort to make it come true. Difficult as it was, it's also been a great deal of fun.

Part II

Organization Dimension: Shaping the Entrepreneurial Organization

5

Leading the Virtual Corporation

William H. Davidow

By projecting ourselves 30 years into the future, we can look back at the decade of the 1990s and see what entrepreneurs can learn from the explosion of technology and its impact. The 1990s ushered in the Information Age, when intangibles such as databases and relationships among companies became more valuable than buildings, factories, and products.

Countries that were 20th century "haves" and 21st century "have nots" were the ones whose governments believed they could handle the technological revolution simply by modifying their existing institutions and processes. The "have" countries were the ones whose governments focused their energies on building advanced communication and transportation systems and training an information technology-literate work force.

The companies that prospered in this period became "virtual corporations," heavily dependent on information products that are easily adaptable to the needs of the user. To become virtual corporations, companies had to reorganize, streamline management, empower employees to make independent decisions, and create long-term relationships with

> employees and clients. These companies' greatest resources were no longer natural ones; rather, the greatest resources became the knowledge inside people's heads. Such companies thrived in countries that created virtual economies and encouraged the growth of virtual corporations.

If we could magically transport ourselves into the future and then look back on the explosion of technology in the 1990s, we could learn many things that would benefit today's entrepreneur. Let's pretend for a moment that it's the year 2015 and we are looking back at the final decade of the 20th century.

One of the first things we would observe is that in the United States in the early 1990s, business labored under the belief that a graceful transition was under way from an industrial society to a post-industrial one, and that the future would be a simple and reasonable extension of the past.

How wrong was this assumption!

From our vantage point in 2015, after 30 years of economic and social shocks, we would see that what actually happened was that business moved from the Industrial Age to the Information Age—and that the differences between life then and now are as great as they were between the 18th and 20th centuries.

THE FIRST GREAT KNOWLEDGE REVOLUTION

In the 1990s, civilization was approximately 75 years into the third great knowledge revolution. The first one occurred 10,000 years ago when hunters and gatherers began applying knowledge to the production of food, creating an agricultural society and making it possible for relatively small areas of land to support large populations.

The resulting population concentrations created the need for the first forms of governments, giving rise to city-states. In Sumeria, storing grains grown in the summer in central locations mandated ownership records, and as a result, the Sumerians learned how to write. Society gradually became stratified, dividing the people who owned land from those who worked on it. Increased productivity brought with it the world's first unemployment problems. Food production in the Nile region was so efficient that there was a surplus of labor. One outcome was the great pyramids—the welfare projects of their time.

What happened in Sumeria illustrates that the application of knowledge is very powerful. Even 10,000 years ago it was capable of transforming the social structure of the world.

THE SECOND GREAT KNOWLEDGE REVOLUTION

Ten thousand years later, the second knowledge revolution occurred when man applied knowledge to the production of goods, giving rise to the Industrial Revolution. The resulting rise in productivity transformed the world. Unprecedented levels of wealth raised the standards of living of the overall population to unimaginable levels. Inexpensive transportation systems made possible efficient world trade, mass production, and suburban populations. Once again, society became stratified, only this time the division was between those who owned and managed the means of production and the factory workers. Nation-states thrived because they were the ideal form of government for an industrialized society.

THE THIRD GREAT KNOWLEDGE REVOLUTION

The dawn of today's Information Age followed quickly on the heels of the Industrial Revolution. Information processing systems have made it possible to control widely dispersed systems by automating the knowledge creation process.

Physical assets have declined in value because, during the final stages of the industrial era, business speculators built too many factories and office buildings and developed too many "me too" products. Now, intangibles are highly valued. Databases, information infrastructures, software, and relationships among companies have become valuable assets. Small companies such as Microsoft have become more valuable than giant corporations such as IBM, Inland Steel, and DuPont.

Once again, society is divided, but this time it is between the educated elite who are the information barons and the information technology illiterates who are the serfs. Governments are no longer nation-states; multinational corporations govern the marketplace. Many individuals, as well as nations, have realized this too late. The result is that many of the 20th century "haves" are now 21st century "have nots," left behind as the newest of the underdeveloped nations.

LOOKING BACK AT THE 1990s

What mistake did these once-powerful and prosperous nations make? Again, let's look at the 1990s from our vantage point in the year 2015. First, we see many governments that believed they could handle the technological revolution simply by modifying their existing institutions and processes. While that had worked in the past, it didn't work this time because these failed governments were totally unprepared to cope with the intangible wealth created by the Information Age. They were designed to deal with the physical, tangible products of the Industrial Age. Their methods of governing were irrelevant or obsolete. Even their languages and measurement tools were useless. Their ability to slow down change so society could adapt to it had been a benefit in the past. Now it was a liability.

One of the first clues that all of this was happening should have been the difficulties and failures encountered by many of the corporate megastars of the 20th century. The giant steel, automotive, computer, retailing, and financial institutions were, in many cases, reduced by corporate downsizing, rightsizing, reorganizing, and reengineering into smaller and emaciated versions of what they had been. The solutions touted by consultants often preserved only temporarily the lives of these terminally ill institutions. Once-great technology leaders ended up as the marketing arms for Third World manufacturers of high technology commodity products.

THE VIRTUAL CORPORATION

We can see that in the 1990s, some of these corporations and many new institutions were able to prosper by adopting a new form of organization made possible by using the tools of the Information Age. They became virtual corporations. The products and services they supplied were virtual products, which, unlike their predecessors in the Industrial Age, were heavily dependent on information content and easily adaptable to the needs of the user. Mass customizing of products—predicted only a decade earlier by Alvin Toffler—had become a viable economic reality. The first virtual products were ones that could be created almost instantaneously at any time, any place, and in any variety. Surprisingly, they often cost less to buy than their mass-produced relatives.

The first virtual product likely was the Polaroid snapshot that appeared in the 1950s. Customers took a photograph and the camera delivered a print in 60 seconds. Kiosks began to appear in shopping centers, offering overnight processing of higher quality conventional photographs. Before long, thanks to low-cost microprocessors, it became possible to deliver color prints to customers within an hour.

The same technology that made these advances possible was soon used to produce electronic cameras and inexpensive color printing systems. Consumers could snap a picture, view the image on their TV set, edit the scene, and print the result in customized photo albums to send to family members around the world.

In our look back at the 1990s, we see that information technology, when combined with organizational innovation, made it possible for the Japanese to produce the three-day car. Customers could send in specifications on Monday and have their new car delivered by Friday. Using similar techniques, a company could accept orders for any one of 100 different castings in the morning, and produce and ship the product to the customer the same day.

Developments in computer-aided design systems made it simple for customers to design the customized products they wanted and transmit the designs to suppliers over high-speed digital networks. These products were often produced in a matter of hours and air freighted that day.

Virtual products were so effective that when they appeared in a given market, they typically destroyed the status quo competition. Perhaps what was more significant was that these new products were able to stand up to low-cost producers in developing countries, and they created value-added products that competed vigorously in world markets. Thus, virtual corporations became the engines of growth for advanced economies. They not only dominated home markets, but export ones as well.

CREATING VIRTUAL PRODUCTS

But creating virtual products wasn't easy. Usually companies had to completely reorganize to do it. It took more than cost cutting and the elimination of middle management to produce the desired results. The initial focus was usually on quality systems. Quick response manufacturing systems required dependable and precise operations. All incoming materials had to be delivered on time and had to be perfect. Factory equipment had to be kept in perfect condition and had to be operational all the time.

Capital equipment breakdowns that plagued many companies in the past were no longer tolerable.

Companies quickly discovered that the management hierarchies that had served modern corporations well for more than 100 years were antiquated. Vertical organizations with unresponsive lines of command could not provide the fast responses required in virtual corporations. Once levels of management were removed, the remaining managers could not supervise everything being done. Employees had to be empowered to take independent action. In order to do this, they had to be trained to make business, engineering, and management decisions.

Of course, it did not make much sense to invest heavily in training employees unless both the companies and the employees were committed to one another for the long term. The companies that succeeded in becoming virtual corporations learned how to create these long-term relationships. They did it by building very high levels of trust between the company and its employees.

THE IMPORTANCE OF INFORMATION TECHNOLOGY

These organizational innovations were only a part of the picture. The backbone of the virtual corporation proved to be its information technology—computer, software, and communication networks. In order to be responsive to market needs, companies had to accumulate and analyze massive amounts of data. It streamed in from point-of-sale terminals, customers surveys, demographic studies, and numerous other sources. Design systems had to be tightly coupled to the factory floor and to the customers' shops, where much of the design was being done. Widely disparate groups which never talked before suddenly found themselves cooperating using group ware technology. Digital networks reached into customers' homes, enabling them to shop in virtual stores in the comfort of their own living rooms.

Virtual corporations had problems maintaining quick-response relationships with transitory customers and began developing personal relationships with customers. This intimate way of working became known as a co-destiny relationship.

Along with the first virtual corporations of the 1990s came chronic high unemployment, triggered when these companies stripped away useless layers of internal bureaucracy. Virtual corporations needed employees who understood information technology. As rapid technological change revolutionized industry, it became clear that it would soon do the same thing to governments, redefining the very idea of nationhood.

Looking back from our vantage point in 2015, surrounded by tribal states and unconsolidated regions, it may be hard to believe that just 30 years ago, nation-states dominated the world. Still, for more than 500 years, nation-states were the best answer to several fundamental political needs. We can see in retrospect that they had three tasks:

1. to preserve themselves and their resources;

2. to protect their citizens;

3. to ensure the economic well-being of those citizens.

Unfortunately, with the end of the Industrial Age, most nations found they could do none of these well. National governments were either too small or too large and always too slow and lumbering to deal with the issues of greatest concern to their citizenry. Self-preservation is an example. As we all know, our current overpopulation disaster had its roots in the 20th century. By the 1990s, with five billion people crowding the globe and another billion being added every decade, it became almost impossible for nations to husband their resources or control immigration, nor did they have the power to deal with this problem on a global basis.

Then they discovered that their greatest resources were no longer natural. Whereas in the Industrial Age the competitive advantage often came from water, farm land, and minerals in the ground, in the Information Age, power came from inside people's heads. Assets that had once been fixed and tangible, such as factories in Manchester and Birmingham, were now intangible. Unlike a factory, a talented person could pack up and move to a new country overnight.

Nations also lost their ability to protect their citizens. Technology put unprecedented power into the hands of individual terrorists who could easily penetrate national borders and create the kind of havoc that once was possible only with an army. At the other extreme, thanks to global communication and the interdependence it fostered, regional disputes engaged the attention of the entire world. One example occurred back in 1991, when the United States, then the most powerful country in the world, enlisted the help of two dozen nations to ensure continuity of its oil supply.

THE ECONOMICS OF THE 1990s

The devastating failures of self-preservation and protection for its citizens suffered by nation-states paled next to the third loss: the loss of economic control.

High speed financial trading, made possible by the rise of telecommunications and computers in the 1970s and 1980s, quickly stripped the ability of countries to manage their own currencies. These same advances also made possible multinational corporations governed by the forces of the market. Their owners and shareholders were largely beyond the reach of national governments. A Chrysler became an American car built in Korea or France. For some, a Toyota was a Japanese car assembled in Great Britain for sale in Germany.

Consequently, by the end of the century those twin towers of the Industrial Age, capital and production, had by and large moved out from under the governance of individual nations. The totalitarian states, such as the Soviet Union, were the first to feel this when they were quickly overrun by technological progress—and collapsed. Capitalist nations were better equipped to cope with transitions; but in time, many of them began to unravel in the face of chronic high unemployment, ethnic strife, a paralysis of government, and sometimes resulting chaos.

While these governments responded with a flurry of programs and laws, they were all futile. Without even knowing it, governments had lost control over their economies, their borders, and ultimately over their nations' futures.

From our perspective of two decades in the future, it is easy for us to see the dilemmas the developed countries of the world faced as they were drained of power. From every direction, ethnic and other special interest groups that were connected by high technology began to detach themselves from the larger society and create de-facto cultural territories. Multinational companies and electronic currency markets carved out entire regions of national economies for their own. To try to regain control, the developed nations ceded their power to supra-national organizations such as the United Nations, the European Community, and the North America Free Trade Zone.

A POPULATION OUT OF CONTROL

Beyond the borders of these developed nations, even more foreboding events were taking place. Of the billion people being added to the global population each decade, most were born in underdeveloped countries. During the Cold War era, one person lived in a developed country for every three who lived in an underdeveloped country. By the end of the century, that ratio was one to four; today, in 2015, it stands at one to six. The "haves" of the world always had a nightmarish vision of the "have-nots" storming the gates. Instead, thanks again to technology, the standard of living for nearly all of the world rose fast enough to placate most of the teeming billions.

Yet it was also technology that impacted the economic depression of the last two decades of the 20th century. Large numbers of workers in underdeveloped nations learned how to assemble technologically sophisticated products. For people used to making $300 per year, the opportunity to learn a skill and make twice that in an electronics factory was the chance of a lifetime. They responded with high-quality products that were at least the equal of those produced in the developed countries—at a fraction of the price.

The resulting economic crisis paralyzed most of the world's developed nations from the late 1980s until the turn of the century. They responded by trying the traditional techniques of setting up tariffs and export controls, managing the currency, and propping up threatened domestic industries. Nothing worked. This was when many governments discovered for the first time that they'd lost control. The citizenry, stunned to find themselves led by a succession of seemingly ineffectual leaders, despaired, raged, or rebelled.

Looking back, we can see that the nations who failed were the ones who tried the same obsolete economic tricks over and over, believing that with just one more tariff or warning to offshore competitors or subsidization that they would turn the corner and restore prosperity.

THE FORMULA FOR SUCCESS

The countries that succeeded and that now lead the world's economy were the ones who recognized early on that the direct, activist means to economic vitality were no longer viable, and that they would have to focus all their energies and resources on becoming more effective. They realized that the mass production of undifferentiated products and services was no longer an effective engine of economic growth. Because every nation in the world quickly had access to every new technological advance, the only competitive advantage left had to come from labor costs—and in that arena, no developed country could possibly compete with an underdeveloped country.

To survive, developed nations needed a new competitive strategy—one that combined products that had a high value-added knowledge content with government programs that created the national infrastructure required for building them. By the early 1990s, every developed country had dozens of virtual corporations capable of competing effectively in world markets. All their governments had to do was focus their energies on building advanced communication and transportation systems and training an information technology-literate work force.

The beauty of these companies—and what made them such powerful economic entities—was that they could only exist in the most advanced economies. They required a sophisticated infrastructure, an educated work force, advanced technology, and highly adaptable organization structures. Some of these factors might be found in a few developing countries, but not all of them together.

And who won? Even Economics 101 students know the answer to that question. The winners were the nations that first grasped the concept of virtual products and encouraged the growth of virtual corporations. They created what economists now call virtual economies. Once they had made the crucial decision to follow this path, the rest followed quickly. They created programs to:

- Improve the national infrastructure through both investment and market incentives;

- Reform the educational system to create an information technology-educated populace;

- Support a strong national technology base, using investment and market incentives;

- Restructure taxes, antitrust laws, securities regulations, and accounting rules to support the creation of knowledge-based businesses.

Looking at this from the year 2015, in the midst of the Information Age, it is easy to think that our 20th century counterparts were thickheaded not to have more quickly identified the solutions to the problems bedeviling their nations. But it is highly likely that each of us, faced with similar circumstances, would have made the same mistakes.

RETURN TO THE PRESENT

Let's come back to the present. Will the scenario I presented actually occur? Much of it is occurring right now and more of it is on the way. Revolutionary advances in technology are always followed by radical changes in the economy and society. Each technological advancement eventually impacts the rest of the world—an exhilarating but also an upsetting truth.

We are living in a remarkable time, one that will culminate in two possible endings: Either increasing chaos and a new kind of Dark Age, or the dawning of another Renaissance far richer in possibilities than the one that occurred 700 years ago.

Creating the economic structure of the 21st century will involve inventing new technologies, applying existing ones more effectively, creating new corporate structures, and developing new products and new services.

What it requires is vision and commitment. *You* can help change the world. *You* can help yourself, your family, your employer, your community, and your nation prepare itself to succeed in the Information Age that is already at hand.

BIBLIOGRAPHY

Chandler, Alfred D., Jr. *The Visible Hand.* Boston: Belknap/Harvard University Press, 1977.

Davidow, William H. *Marketing High Technology: An Insider's View.* New York: The Free Press, 1986.

Davidow, William H., and Michael S. Malone. *The Virtual Corporation.* New York: Harper Collins, 1992.

Davidow, William H., and Bro Uttal. *Total Customer Service: The Ultimate Weapon.* New York: Harper & Row, 1989.

Reich, Robert. *The Next American Frontier.* New York: Times Books, 1983.

Rheingold, Howard. *Virtual Reality.* New York: Summit Books, 1991.

Toffler, Alvin. *The Third Wave.* New York: William Morrow, 1980.
Womack, James P., Daniel T. Jones, and Daniel Roos. *The Machine That Changed the World.* New York: Rawson Associates/Macmillan, 1990.

6

Playing the Great Game of Business: Open-Book Management and Leaders

John P. Stack

Jack Stack was working at International Harvester in 1983 when it became clear that his division, Springfield Remanufacturing Corporation (SRC), was about to fold. SRC was purchased through a management buy-out, and today, thanks to playing what they call the Great Game of Business, SRC has enjoyed unparalleled success.

Knowing that a healthy balance sheet results from a healthy work environment, the new officers decided that the best way to tackle the dual problems of cash and morale was to tell everyone who worked at the plant exactly where the company stood financially and how individual workers could impact the bottom line. In short, everyone would be treated like owners. This empowered employees and helped them understand the "Big Picture." The officers also worked at boosting company pride through social and sporting events, competitions, open houses, and various kinds of internal rewards.

Management's role was to act as a cheerleader and keep everyone on target. Direct supervision was eliminated. The result was a strong sense of unity and a "can do" environment in which people worked their hardest and also had fun. Workers felt secure because they took responsibility for the business and shared in the rewards.

The Great Game of Business is a system of open-book management that was born in 1983 when Springfield Remanufacturing Corporation (SRC) was about to die.

SRC was originally a division of International Harvester. Several of the managers at SRC had worked with Harvester in its Melrose Park, Illinois plant for 10 years or more—starting in entry level positions and eventually running operations. The general economic conditions in the early 1980s brought rough times to International Harvester, and as a result, outlying divisions, like SRC, faced being sold or closed. More than 120 people at SRC did not want to see it go under, and as a result the management and employees made an offer to buy SRC from Harvester. To do so, $9 million was needed to buy the plant. Managers and employees were able to scrape together $100,000 and borrowed the rest, and in February 1983 became the new owners. They knew it was like putting down $1,000 to buy a $90,000 house: You don't really own it—the bank does, and it will pull the plug the first time a payment is missed.

In business terms, SRC had an 89-to-1 debt-to-equity ratio and was nearly comatose as a corporate entity. The bank was so concerned about the debt position that they set up an office right in the plant to watch what went on day-to-day. All the assets of the company were mortgaged in order to pay on the negotiated buying price of $9 million with an interest rate of 18 percent. A $10,000 mistake would kill the business—monthly debt payments were $90,000!

SRC has celebrated its 10th birthday. It has expanded to include three major divisions and 10 offshoot companies. In addition, the number of employees has grown from 120 in 1983 to more than 600 at the present.

Today SRC remanufactures engines and engine components from cars, bulldozers, and 18-wheelers. The process includes saving the parts that are in good shape, repairing those that are damaged, and replacing those that are beyond repair.

SRC also does something else: The firm teaches people about business so they can succeed. This is done by providing the necessary knowledge to allow people to play the "Game." The Game is "The Great Game of Business"—a system of open-book management that is the reason SRC has survived and thrived beyond expectation.

HOW THE GREAT GAME OF BUSINESS WAS BORN

In the process of raising funds to purchase SRC, 50 American financial institutions turned down the loan. Fortunately, one accepted. During the process, we learned that a business is not judged by quality, customer service, or costs, but by the health of its balance sheets.

We were amazed that the people we approached about a loan controlled hundreds of millions of dollars and thousands upon thousands of jobs (and so controlled many people's lives), yet did not have the responsibilities of meeting payroll, improving customer service, or designing a vision. They merely judged a company on how well it was performing within a specific set of financial ratios.

We already knew that a healthy balance sheet resulted from a healthy work environment. To increase productivity, we had to eliminate every problem we could on the line. That's when we started making some decisions that became the framework for the Great Game of Business.

LEARNING TO PLAY THE GAME

The first decision was that the best way to cope with the dual problems of cash and morale was to make sure everyone knew the company's financial pulse every step of the way. This meant telling the people where the cash was and then getting them involved in deciding what to do with it.

The open-book management system, in effect, delegated to employees the responsibility for their own job security. Everyone who worked in the company received a "scorecard," which was access to all company financial records and a way to influence the score. They could see for themselves how safe their jobs were and what they could do to make them safer. This didn't provide guarantees—which don't exist anywhere anymore—but it gave them a say in how the business was run.

Access to information about the company did something else as well: It made people feel they had a career, not just a job. They came to the plant each day with enthusiasm because they had responsibilities and could make decisions. They knew their opinions mattered and that they, in effect, ran the company. This developed leaders—employees in control of their own destinies as well as their company's destiny. They had the Big Picture in mind as they went about their everyday business.

What resulted was a strong sense of unity. Everyone in the company knew what was going on. Everyone played by the same rules. Everyone worked hard—and everyone had fun. The employees were focused and worked as a team. Playing the Game created an organization where people developed a sense of security by taking responsibility for the business, their performance, and their own levels of success. SRC succeeded by giving each employee a voice in how the company could be run and a stake in the financial outcome.

THE RULES OF THE GAME

The Great Game of Business is a system of open-book management where every person in a company learns how to read and operate from financial statements. Employees understand the Big Picture before they ever perform a job function so that they understand how the company makes money and what is done with that money. The income statement and balance sheets guide daily business.

The Game has 10 basic laws or rules:

1. You get what you give.
2. It's easy to stop one person, but it's difficult to stop 100.
3. What goes around, comes around.
4. You do what you gotta do.
5. You gotta wanna.
6. You can sometimes fool the fans, but you can never fool the players.
7. When you raise the bottom, the top rises.
8. When people set their own targets, they usually hit them.
9. If nobody pays attention, people stop caring.
10. Change begins at the top.

And there's one more—the ultimate higher law: when you appeal to the highest level of thinking, you get the highest level of performance.

APPLYING THE RULES AT SRC

Every person at SRC, from the janitors on the shop floor to the highest managers, knows all about the business. They know that the two most critical factors are making money and generating cash. Financial statements—or "numbers"—are used to keep score on the financial progress at every level of the company. Every SRC employee has access to the "numbers" every day. Nobody has to rely on second-hand information. It's a philosophy based on the belief that the more people know about a company, the better that company will perform. The key to success in business is sharing information with the people who contribute to that success.

Such action closes the gap between management and workers, creating a company where all workers think and act like owners. At SRC, an Employee Stock Ownership Plan (ESOP) makes all employees owners of the company. SRC also has a bonus plan that honors hard work by teams, paying off when quarterly and annual targets are met. Everybody knows the targets, everybody works toward the same goals, and everybody thinks of themselves as important wheels in the company machine—because they are!

YOU NEED SOMETHING MORE

As good as it sounds, it takes more than an ESOP or a bonus program to get people to think and act like owners. They will still rely on management for direction. But if you give them access to the company's financials, you will encourage them to think, meet goals, plan for the future, and see their own place in that future.

Our people not only know where the company is going, but what they and their teammates must do to get it there. They can handle challenges on the shop floor as well as in the conference room because they know their target. It is their company. It is their future.

Playing the Game eliminates the "entitlement thinking" that has hurt so many American businesses. No one at SRC is entitled to anything. All work toward common goals and earn every success and bonus the company enjoys. Working together makes the company run.

BEFORE YOU CAN BEGIN TO PLAY

Before the Great Game of Business can be played, two conditions must exist in your company:

Management Must Have Credibility

Without it, people won't listen to you, and they won't believe the numbers you give them. They'll think bonus programs or other games are gimmicks to get them to work harder for less money so that you can get richer. Employees must feel that management is sensitive to them and their problems, that their contributions are valued and that management is fair. They must be willing to give you the benefit of the doubt.

To do this, listen to your people. Bring them into your office in small groups and ask them what they want from the business and from themselves, and what they want for their futures. Then listen to them. Apply their concerns to the way your company does business. Make the changes visible.

Most important of all, be willing to transfer to individuals the responsibility for their own success. They must be willing to accept that responsibility. They gotta wanna!

Employees Must Have Fire in Their Eyes

No company can play the Great Game of Business unless employees feel like winners. The fire in people's eyes can be kindled by setting up win/win situations. Give them goals to work for by putting together some production-oriented games, some safety-oriented targets, or some new-customer numbers they can shoot for. These will stimulate interest in coming to work every day to see how well they performed the previous day. When employees feel like winners, they care about what they produce. They care about their fellow workers. They care about meeting goals.

A technique that accomplished the caring attitude at SRC started with a weekend open house in the employee parking lot at the Melrose Park facility. Tractors were placed in the parking lot and the employees invited their families and friends to see where they worked. People feel important when they can show others where they work and what they do.

People were given buckets of paint and encouraged to decorate their machines and work areas. Some painted bold statements on the walls. Signs and symbols were everywhere—American flags, Hell's Angels insignias, and everything else you can imagine. Some departments put up slogans such as "Machining: We Make It Work!" Nothing was color-coordinated, and it looked awful, but it was theirs. They were putting their own identities out there for everyone to see. When they brought in their families, they could say, "Here's where I work. This is my environment."

Many SRC-sponsored activities generated pride. These ranged from fishing tournaments to baseball tournaments and local contests for charity. SRC employees also participated in relay races against other companies.

SRC sponsored at least one major event each month. The approach was to compete as a team, to win as a team, and to be rewarded as individual team members.

Today, our employees are used to being winners. They continue to work hard with a sense of pride and ownership through our bonus program, ESOP, weekly staff meetings, and the games we play around the numbers. Our goal continues to be to improve everyone's standard of living by creating wealth and distributing it back through the company. The secret of productivity is to develop an organization whose people feel good about themselves—so good, in fact, that they want to help others.

THE IMPORTANCE OF TEAM WORK

In the Great Game of Business, we recognize that business is a team sport. The daily, weekly, monthly, and quarterly goals are built around team work. When a problem occurs in the company, team members decide what to do and how to do it to solve the problem. Management's role is to make sure everyone is playing by the same rule book and that they all know the winning target. Management must also act as cheerleaders and keep team members motivated if the going gets tough. When the goal is reached, management recognizes and rewards team effort. It's no surprise that teams will not only wipe out a problem but will often improve upon the situation.

SHARING THE BIG PICTURE

Practicing open-book management has been the key to SRC's success—success based on employees knowing and sharing information, ideas, and numbers. Making the Big Picture a constant focus has kept all the hourly, daily, and weekly tasks in line and given them importance as a means to an end.

Companies frequently forget to share the Big Picture with employees. Unless employees know what they're working toward and how they fit into the scheme, there's no way they can feel like part of the team. That's why SRC has opened the books and taught the numbers. Our people use the numbers as tools to help them do their work every day. The numbers link the individual to the Big Picture and are a constant reminder of where each person, each department, and the company as a whole is headed.

It's true that information is power. In the Great Game of Business, power is not limited to the management level—it's in everyone's hands. That way, all benefit.

MAKING OPEN-BOOK MANAGEMENT WORK FOR YOU

Many people have asked how to become open-book managers and how to play the Great Game of Business. These questions are answered in the book *The Great Game of Business: The Only Sensible Way to Run a Company.* In a nutshell, here's a blueprint for action for open book management:

- **Start with the Income Statement.** It's the best way to draw people into the Game because it demonstrates cause and effect. It can be used to monitor what's happening and to show people their role in affecting the outcome.

- **Highlight the categories where you spend the most money.** They have the greatest impact on profit, so monitor them very closely.

- **Break down categories into controllable elements.** If labor is a variable expense, people should see it vary. If trucks are used in the business, people should know how much they cost. In a sales organization, it's important to keep a close eye on travel, entertainment, and other selling expenses. In a professional service firm, show billable hours. The idea is to set up the income statement in a way that allows people to observe the effects of what they do.

- **Use the income statement to educate people about the balance sheet.** While the action may center around the income statement, it is the balance sheet that tells the real score—how secure jobs are, how much wealth has been created, and where the company is vulnerable. Once people understand the income statement, they can see how changes on it affect the balance sheet.

Financial statements should be set up so they communicate. Use the statement the banker uses to assess the business as a basis for creating your own customized statement. Show more detail than the bank statement and itemize the company's budgets and costs, then all employees will understand how they fit into the Big Picture.

At SRC, each line item on our financial statements has a person's name attached to it. That way, everyone knows the numbers for which they are responsible.

It takes some time to create the best statement. Start with the basics: Where is the cash? Where are the inventories? Where are the receivables? How much is owed to others? Then as people begin to ask questions, expand the financial statements, and categorize and provide detail according to the company's needs.

COMMUNICATION IS VITAL

Communicate the information on a regular basis. Open-book management doesn't work unless communication is strong. At SRC, open meetings are held every Wednesday at 9 a.m. It's called "The Great Huddle." The managers and supervisors who attend then hold a series of "Chalk Talks" with their departments and divisions, guaranteeing that everyone in the company has the weekly numbers within 48 hours of the Wednesday morning huddle.

In the meetings, the numbers are discussed, then reassessed according to the results of the previous week and what is predicted for the next week, month, and six months. Strategies are planned. Actions are outlined. When the meeting ends, everyone knows who is where, how the game is unfolding, and what each has to do to keep moving the company closer to the goal line. Don't underestimate the power and importance of these regular meetings. They are the most valuable communication link and are vital to the success of the firm.

WHY THE GREAT GAME IS A WINNER

The Great Game of Business is so logical! It eliminates direct supervision from management. People are motivated because they have been shown how to put money in their pockets. Instead of threats and intimidation, people are motivated by becoming a vital part of the company.

WHERE IS SRC TODAY?

People at SRC are the proof of the "ultimate higher law"; which is, appeal to the highest level of thinking to get the highest level of performance. The people of SRC think like the business leaders and owners that they are. They are self-reliant. They control their own destinies. They don't have to be told to work as a team—they ARE a team! The smooth functioning of the teams combined with the ever-questioning nature of humans who love to learn has brought SRC to a point of decentralizing. A number of small, spin-off entrepreneurial companies are being led by enterprising SRC employees.

Decentralization also helps in playing the Game better. As the whole breaks into smaller units, communication is more manageable and teams remain a close-knit, workable size. Decentralization discourages the de facto bureaucracy that seems to accompany large corporations.

Today, SRC is a diversified collection of enterprises and an ongoing business incubator. By and large, the new companies are being run by people who have come up through the ranks at SRC. As hourly workers, salaried professionals, and middle managers, these people rode the roller-coaster in the 1980s, learning all about the Great Game of Business in the process. Their leadership abilities were fine-tuned as they learned to play the Game. Now they are ready to apply what they've learned to enterprises of their own. They will have the opportunity to acquire the businesses in the future, whenever they choose. Meanwhile, SRC will keep on spinning off new ones.

Frankly, SRC now has more opportunities than can be accommodated. Businesses are waiting to be launched. The remanufacture of a trouble-some engine component turned a $500,000-per-year problem into a company with annual revenues of $2.5 million. Two other firms were started to help solve problems for two major customers, Navistar and J.I. Case. SRC has even begun a seminar business in response to people from other companies who want to know how to play the Game.

It's only right that these businesses should form. When employees are empowered, the next logical step is to help them become business owners. It's like planting a fruit tree: You plant the seed, tend it, work with it, and watch it grow strong. You continue to encourage its growth, and it produces fruit. From that fruit come more seeds, which are in turn planted, tended, and nurtured. SRC has been fortunate enough to provide fertile ground for what is becoming an orchard of strong, vital businesses.

THE BOTTOM LINE: WHAT'S IN IT FOR YOUR COMPANY?

No one would have believed 10 years ago that SRC would be at its current level of expansion and profitability.

From 1983 to 1986, sales grew by more than 30 percent per year, and earnings went from a loss of $60,488 in the first year to pre-tax earnings of $2.7 million (7 percent of sales) in our fourth. Not a single person has ever been laid off, not even when a contract representing 40 percent of the business was lost for a whole year. By 1991, annual sales were almost $70 million, and the work force had increased to about 650 people.

But perhaps the most impressive number centers on the value of SRC stock, worth $.10 a share at the time of the buyout. By the end of January 1991, that $.10 share had soared in value to $18.20, an increase of 18,200 percent in eight years! As a result, hourly workers who had been with SRC from the beginning had holdings in the employee stock ownership plan worth as much as $35,000 per person—almost the price of a home in Springfield, Missouri.

These numbers are not provided to boast or to brag. They are provided to show the true value of involving people in the Great Game of Business. Playing the Game helps make the company stronger and more successful. When the people are empowered, there's no room for petty grievances and turf wars. All play the Game together—playing by the same rules, running plays from the same playbook, heading toward the same goal line.

The going can get tough, but it's never boring. The team is always working together, always finding ways to have a good time while working hard. It's a system that makes sense; in fact, it's based on business principles that have been around for more than 100 years. SRC just dusted off the ideas and incorporated them into the way we do business today.

America's greatest hope for the future is its people. When people are taught how to play the Game, they excel. When people excel, the business excels. And as more companies learn to value human potential, the face of American business is going to change. America will once again be able to enjoy greatness. Future generations will be left with a legacy of a strong work ethic, pride in a job well done, and the example of individual strength working within a unified team.

It's all in the attitude. It's all in the numbers. It's all in the Game.

BIBLIOGRAPHY

Stack, Jack. *The Great Game of Business.* New York: Currency Books, 1992.

7

Building the High-Performance Company: The Entrepreneurial Challenge

Robert Rosen

As America's corporate atmosphere undergoes rapid change, the entrepreneurs most likely to succeed are the ones who embrace change and who understand the human aspects of business. They know that healthy people make healthy companies, and that healthy companies have the best chance of being profitable.

Companies must take a holistic approach to employee health. If they do this and have a healthy work force, their workers will reward their companies with loyalty, hard work, and longevity.

Six principles guide the creation of a healthy company, including these four:

- The power of respect is greater than the power of money.
- Wise leaders know how to follow.
- If you don't manage change, it will manage you.
- Healthy people are assets that appreciate in value.

Entrepreneurs who create a pro-worker environment, who

are committed to strong families, who set a good example themselves, and who embrace diversity will be the leaders of American business in the year 2000. The great challenge to entrepreneurs is to create organizations espousing these values. These healthy companies can only be built by people who live by these values themselves and who have the vision to create a world in which these values flourish.

The words "entrepreneur" and "American Dream" both conjure up visions of endless possibility, equal access, and the pursuit of happiness. They also mean the opportunity to take a chance—and that's how many American success stories begin.

Skeptics may doubt, but there's never been a better time to be an entrepreneur than now, when many industries are downsizing and reorganizing, leaving room for entrepreneurs who can reinvent the way America does business.

This climate offers entrepreneurs both challenges and opportunities. They have the challenges of rapid change and personal sacrifices, and the messiness of starting a business, combined with the opportunity to transform the American corporate landscape.

The entrepreneurs most likely to succeed are the ones who embrace change and who understand themselves and the human aspects of their enterprises. They are willing to share power and to empower others.

They understand that healthy people make healthy companies, and that healthy companies have the best chance of being profitable.

Here is a description of such a company.

THE HEALTHY COMPANY

Imagine a company that truly cares about its employees. In this company, the employees reciprocate with hard work and loyalty. They are constantly looking for ways to improve their skills and to deliver a better product or a faster service. Their easy banter shows they enjoy what they're doing. The office is filled with voices that are sincere, warm, and personal.

Perhaps most remarkable is that the employees respect one another and graciously share ideas with one another. In place of the me-versus-you antagonism found in so many companies, there is a sense of teamwork and tolerance.

This sketch of a healthy company may sound far-fetched, but in reality, many companies today operate like this. They have a competitive advantage over the oppressive, fear-driven companies that have dominated American business for generations, because at the core of their corporate culture is a humanistic approach to all the people who work there. Such a company is guided by the following values.

- **Commitment to Self-Knowledge and Development.** Employees who are encouraged to explore personal growth will take risks and try new approaches to problem solving.

- **Firm Belief in Decency.** Everyone in the company practices the Golden Rule—not just in theory, but in fact.

- **Respect for Individual Differences.** Rather than insisting that everyone stick to a "cultural norm," employees and managers respect the richness of diversity and the imaginative ideas dissimilar people bring to their jobs.

- **Spirit of Partnership.** Everyone, from the CEO on down, believes in forming strong relationships. They understand the dynamics of giving and taking, leading and following. People see themselves as part of a team.

- **High Priority for Health and Well-Being.** The healthy company offers workers adequate health care coverage, assistance programs, flexible scheduling, family-leave policies, competitive and equitable pay, and profit sharing.

- **Appreciation of Flexibility and Resilience.** The healthy company gives employees the tools to adapt to change, providing them with advance notice of layoffs, and making displacements and transitions as smooth as possible.

- **Passion for Products and Process.** Employees *care* what happens to their company. They feel personally responsible for its successes and failures. They know that profit is not the immediate goal; rather, it is the result of doing everything else right.

The Six Core Principles of the Healthy Company

These values are bound to each other in a holistic tapestry. They guide the progress of the healthy company and are intertwined with the following six core principles.

1. THE POWER OF RESPECT IS GREATER THAN THE POWER OF MONEY

While corporate America gives considerable lip service to the term "respect," in the daily workings of the average company it is at best represented only in slogans and is mostly ignored. Business pays a high price for this disrespect: poor morale, high turnover, and an inability to attract quality employees. Drug abuse, theft, and sabotage are among the more serious consequences of resentful employees who know they don't have their company's respect. The costs, in real terms, can be high.

To build respect throughout the company, management must explore the values and assumptions employees bring to work with them every day, look at how employees relate to each other, and then decide what changes would create a more respectful environment. With that done, management must then strive to develop the following qualities in the company work force.

Trust

This consists of:

- Credibility—You do what you say you'll do.
- Dependability—You meet your deadlines.
- Predictability—You refrain from tantrums and sudden policy shifts.
- Value of the common good—You put aside self-interest to further a project.
- Emotional safety—You don't abuse people.

Management instills trust in workers by:

- Setting an example—You talk to other employees about trust.
- Surveying the level of trust in the office—You determine if any gossip or sniping is occurring.
- Sharing information—You talk openly with employees about the health of the company.

- Looking for opportunities to explain your personal motives—You acknowledge that you are working toward the same goal.

- Avoiding personal criticisms and favors—You do not criticize, nor do you create favorites and have cliques.

Appreciation for the Human Element

Many companies think all their employees want is more money and better benefits. In reality, what employees want most is respect for everything they do, from their thoughts and fears, to their desire to learn, to their personal and family lives. Rather than respect, most employees encounter profound indifference from their employers.

Management can show appreciation by gestures and words, and through the giving of tangible rewards. To effectively show appreciation:

- Ask your employees what excites them.

- Get to know someone else's job.

- Show your appreciation publicly.

- Reward hard work with fiscal incentives, such as performance bonuses or stock options.

Communication

To show respect for employees, managers must put aside their personal agendas and listen intently to what people want from their work. Then they should provide feedback. To improve communication:

- Open your eyes and ears, and listen to the entire person. Body language communicates many things people are reluctant to say. When talking to employees, try to avoid distractions such as phone calls. Be patient. Good communication takes time.

- Say what you mean by striving to avoid bureaucratic jargon that can depersonalize communication. Employees are frequently left hanging, trying to decipher what's been said to them. With communication, more is better and much more is best.

- Encourage feedback by evaluating employee performance in a predictable, private, and nonconfrontational manner.

- Tame office conflict. If a problem exists, acknowledge it. Declare your intention to find a solution. Break the conflict into smaller parts and try not to let immediate emotions escalate the conflict.

Ethics

Ethics is basically the issue of fairness: fair promotions, fair benefits, and hearings. This means giving as much weight to people concerns as you would to economic concerns. To instill ethics in your company, practice the following:

- Align your personal and business ethics. You should have a single code of ethics for all situations. Before making any business decision, ask yourself, "Would I want to explain this to my family or see it in the paper?"

- Set your ethical climate. Draft a code of ethics for your immediate workplace. Identify ethical conflict as early as possible. Reward ethical behavior and discipline unethical behavior. Institute safe channels for employees to address unfair work practices, and ask prospective employees about their ethics.

Remember, respect is a right and a responsibility. Respect will flourish where wise leaders walk the walk, not just talk the talk.

2. WISE LEADERS KNOW HOW TO FOLLOW

As we all know, management-labor relations have a hostile history in this country. To this day, laborers and executives continue to slug it out, with the workplace often serving as the battleground. This fractious behavior is not unlike that of a dysfunctional family: Employees behave like unruly adolescents, managers like incompetent parents, and companies like strict, severe patriarchs.

In a healthy company, rigid controls are replaced by empowerment. Responsibility and authority are shared by all. This kind of enlightened leadership is guided by several truths:

- Influence is earned, not seized. It is the result of hard work and comes from the earned respect of others.

- Leaders are defined by their followers. True leaders are elevated from the pack by their colleagues. They achieve leadership because it is granted to them.

- Leadership springs from accepting imperfection. People want to follow other people—imperfect and human.

- Power increases as you give it away. Sharing power prevents stupid mistakes.

- Power built on fear is an expression of impotence, not leadership. Fear and ego cannot replace strength and character.

- No matter how bright your reflection, it will always fade away. Good leaders avoid the distractions of fame.

To put leadership into practice, follow these seven directives:

- Tailor your leadership skills. Each situation will require a different set of skills. What is inspiring leadership for one employee may be insulting to another.

- Open yourself to feedback. Soliciting ideas from others often requires that you give up some control and that you be open to personal criticism. But the benefits of such an open-door policy in terms of respect and employee morale are worth pursuing.

- Symbolize your beliefs. Sweeping actions representing your leadership, as long as they are sincere, can serve as important markers to others. They send clear signals about what you believe is important.

- Reject showy signs of power. Avoid ostentatious displays of wealth, layers of personal staff, or a specialized vocabulary few people understand.

- Give people the tools to lead. These include information, skills, responsibility, control, and awards.

- Let people run with good ideas. If you encourage experimenting with ideas and taking risks, excitement and innovation will follow.

- Encourage acts of civil disobedience. Learning to fight for ideas and allowing others to do so is a trait well worth cultivating. It encourages in-house entrepreneurs.

Developing an empowered workplace involves flattening the pyramid into circles and teams. Successful teams are self-managing, and they share control, influence, and consequences. Teams must be willing to learn. Members must be open to diverse viewpoints.

Sharing company information is a vital part of enlightened leadership. As much as possible, enlightened leaders share all pertinent information with everyone, creating a sense of responsibility and trust.

Healthy companies are guided by people who cultivate and celebrate new ideas. Properly heeded, these ideas will become self-perpetuating: Employees know the company listens to their suggestions because they see them implemented, which then inspires more ideas.

This new concept of leadership applies the principles of participation, teamwork, and ownership to every level of the company. It fosters input and involvement from employees on a range of company-wide concerns. It breaks the dysfunctional chain that has shackled the workplace for generations. It is part of the sea of change sweeping through American business.

3. IF YOU DON'T MANAGE CHANGE, IT WILL MANAGE YOU

Constant change in the workplace is now the norm. Companies and people must change if they are to become healthier and more productive. The first step for the manager is to understand how they themselves react to change. Ideally, change should be regarded as a challenge, not a disaster. You should attempt to develop these four qualities:

- Understanding. Knowing the ramifications of change in all areas of the workplace.
- Flexibility. The ability to adjust, make compromises, learn new skills, and adapt to new surroundings.
- Resilience. Developing the self-confidence to weather stressful situations, knowing you will bounce back.
- Momentum. Moving through change with steady forward motion.

The Entrepreneur as Guide

Your role as an entrepreneurial leader is that of a guide. As you guide employees through periods of change, consider these suggestions:

- **Tailor Your Actions to the Change.** Changes that affect the whole company require a full panoply of communication skills; slow, incremental changes require a methodical, step-by-step approach.

- **Overcome Your Personal Obstacles.** A manager without focus will overlook the human crisis in times of change and only see the tangible, physical changes. The healthy company comes to terms with the emotional consequences of change.

- **Use Values As Your Guide.** Strong company values clearly expressed are the best asset in times of change. They provide employees with the assurance that no matter what happens, the company will continue to treat them fairly and respectfully.

Coping with Change: Three Stages

As people cope with change, they generally pass through three stages: denial, resistance, and exploration.

Denial

At the outset of change, employees often experience an overwhelming sense of imminent loss—of security, of belonging, of direction, and of their own competence. They may express their denial in numbness, apathy, and the wishful assumption that it will "all go away." One way to cope with denial is to honor the past and let employees know that change doesn't negate past achievements; rather, it celebrates them. The second way is to inform regularly. You do this by feeding employees constant, accurate information during times of change.

Resistance

Complaining and foot-dragging are unpleasant but natural reactions to change. The manager in a healthy company acknowledges the validity of these feelings. Employee resistance can be soothed by sharing your vision. You do this by inviting employees to see the larger picture and by describing the future you see for your company. Also, don't make promises you can't keep. Don't tell people their jobs are safe unless you mean it. The price you pay for dishonesty will be higher than the discomfort of frank communication.

Exploration

Eventually, the work force in a healthy community advances through change to the level of exploration. At this stage, the manager needs to help employees stay focused. This can be done by involving employees in the mechanics. Arrange meetings to solicit suggestions and opinions, and let people make some decisions and carry out critical assignments.

Pay attention to symbols. They take on special significance in times of change. Visible signs of change like new paint or new logos help people recognize the change around them. Your goal is for employees to arrive at a new commitment, using change as a catalyst for heightened productivity and more challenge.

Entrepreneurs must learn these new approaches if they are to adapt to the changing landscape of American business. Doing so is critical to the healthy company.

4. LIFETIME LEARNING PAYS LIFELONG DIVIDENDS

Continual self-evaluation is vital to the healthy company. At every level, skills and knowledge must be evaluated and refined to keep pace with change and maintain a competitive edge. Organizational learning enables companies to solve their own problems and build their own futures. For a company to do this, employees must have these core competencies.

- **The Ability to Learn.** Do your workers continuously acquire new skills? Do they know how to process new information? The ability to recognize patterns, test hypotheses, and learn from trial-and-error problem solving are vital qualities of the employee of the healthy company.

- **Techno-knowledge.** Technical skills and knowledge enable people to handle a broad spectrum of information, including written literacy, computer literacy, and basic math skills.

- **People Skills.** In the healthy company, people communicate with individuals who think and work in noticeably different ways.

- **Emotional Literacy.** The ability to acknowledge and respond to the feelings of others is no longer a "soft" skill but a requirement in the workplace of the future.

- **Intuitive Abilities.** The healthy company attracts people who are comfortable relying on hunches and who dispense with normal linear thinking and have visionary insights about the future.

- **Personal Management.** Employees in healthy companies have the ability to cope with personal problems and stresses in an ordered way.

A huge gap exists between what American businesses currently practice and the adoption of these core competencies. This gap is the result of a stagnated learning culture in this country. We see learning as a phase of one's youth rather than a lifetime pursuit. The goal is to transform the workplace into an environment where learning is seen as the key to enduring success.

The first step begins with you. You are responsible for your own personal and professional development. You should develop a plan for yourself that includes these six goals:

- **Discover Your Personal Vision.** Why are you doing what you do? What is important to you personally and how is this manifested in your work?
- **Establish Professional Goals.** If your personal vision is the dream, then your goals are the road map to turn that dream into reality.
- **Identify Your Knowledge Gaps.** Be honest about what you know and don't know.
- **Seek Out Mentors.** Watching how a person you admire handles personal and professional situations can be invaluable help.
- **Pursue New Interests Outside of Work.** What you learn in a variety of experiences will enrich your work in surprising ways.
- **Turn Mistakes into Opportunities.** Mistakes help you learn what you know versus what you need to know.

Learning in the Workplace

Once you complete this personal inventory, you can turn your attention to how your employees learn. Here are some ways you can act as a guide for your employees, reinvigorating the learning process in the workplace.

- **Conduct Personal Career Audits.** Begin by considering each employee's education and experience. Identify what they each bring to the job. Focus on that knowledge and their performance. Ask how each of them measures up to the tasks they have been assigned. Once you have done this, you will want to think about potential and possibilities. What could this person be doing in two years' time?

- **Formulate an Individual Learning Plan.** You and each employee should set goals specifically tailored to the employee's strengths. Extra education, experience in other areas, and assuming more responsibility might be parts of this kind of plan.

- **Teach People How to Learn.** Transform the daily tasks of the work force into opportunities for learning. This may involve changing some habits so that the free exchange of ideas can take place on a regular basis.

- **Master the Mentoring Process.** A mentor can be an indispensable model for the principles of the healthy company, teaching such intangibles as humility, patience, respect for other's perspectives, and a more humane approach to other people.

A healthy company creates an arena where employees can improve upon their talents. They feel comfortable taking chances, making mistakes, and testing new skills. Becoming an institution where learning takes place means your company fosters personal and professional development at every level and for all employees.

These are some strategies corporations use to encourage learning.

Get Serious About Training

It is estimated that by the year 2000, 75 percent of all employees will need retraining. Leading edge companies are ready for this because:

- They invest three to five percent of payroll in education.

- They link business strategy and training goals.

- They try whatever works—formal courses, seminars, internal training, consultants, etc.

Open a Skills Bank

Skills banks have information about new jobs in the company, what skills the company has in its work force to cover these jobs, and what retraining will be needed.

Reward Learners

Rewards reinforce the process-first attitude that is central to healthy learning environments. It says real development, not office politics, leads to advancement.

Institutionalize Learning Stretches

These are activities and projects that allow employees to expand their skills and, in the process, to discover new rewards in their work environment. The challenge is to find the right stretch at the right time. The best time is when the employee has learned 80 percent of his/her current job. Examples of learning stretches are:

- Fast track advances—special programs for high-potential employees.
- Alternative assignments—rotating employees through various departments so they can receive training in all of them.
- Alternative career paths—attractive lateral moves within a corporation if there is a log-jam at the top.

Counsel the Working Wounded

Talk frankly with employees about their discontent. Look for ways to restructure their jobs to enhance their sense of accomplishment and desire to learn.

Create Educational Partnerships

Students in the workplace will always stimulate the learning process. They also become a pre-trained work force, familiar with the demands of your company.

Learning is a lifelong process. As an entrepreneur, you will be learning continuously as you navigate uncharted waters. The healthy company affirms this process, just as it affirms the health of its work force.

5. OUR STRENGTHS LIE IN CELEBRATING DIFFERENCES

In 1988, white males comprised 45 percent of the work force. By the year 2000, that number will shrink to 23 percent. At the same time, female workers will increase from 45 percent to 64 percent of the work force, and non-whites from 14 percent to almost 40 percent.

Unfortunately, the typical workplace is not prepared for this multicultural reality. We continue to adhere to values created by the white man's power structure that often subdue, dominate, and control. They tend to celebrate stoic self-reliance and regard any emotional communication as suspect. They tend to be rigid, hierarchical, and formal, discouraging disagreement and shunning non-conformist opinions. The clash between this outdated value system and today's diverse work force is manifest in company publications written in sexist language, ignoring holidays important to "minority" workers, and/or not considering older workers for promotion.

In a healthy company, individual differences are not only tolerated, they are encouraged and supported. The healthy company realizes that as the work force diversifies, so does the market. It welcomes a rich cross-section of Americans into its work force so it can better serve the market to which it sells.

Creating a diverse work force and promoting tolerance for diverse values is not only humanistic, but is sound business as well.

Nurturing a Diverse Work Force

As the leader of a company, you are responsible for promoting tolerance and diversity. Begin by examining your own prejudices. You will find that most prejudice is based in fear and ignorance. For example, we reject strangers because we don't know them. Here are some suggestions for overcoming prejudices:

- Examine your own cultural roots. What are the common generalizations people make about your background?

- Watch carefully how you ascribe personality traits to other groups. Do you exclude them in subtle ways?

- Ask yourself what assumptions are behind these stereotypes. Are your feelings based on first-hand experience or hearsay?

- Try to imagine what life would be like in someone else's shoes. How does this person's actual experience differ from your initial suppositions?

In order to promote tolerance in the workplace, a manager should try to utilize to the greatest degree possible the diverse talents people offer. Here are some ways you can handle the complexities of your diverse work force.

Conduct a Cultural Audit

Survey the people who work for you to see what you've been missing. Consider these four things:

- **Demographics:** Gender, race, sexual orientation, primary language, age, cultural heritage.
- **Personal characteristics:** Marital status, number of children, family circumstances, personal interests.
- **Working styles:** Desire for flexibility, need for independence, willingness to travel.
- **Lifestyle values:** Neatness, practicality, loyalty, sense of humor, spirituality.

Recognize the Faces of Diversity

Here are some concerns various groups may have:

- **Women.** On average, a woman earns 70 percent of what a man earns. Are your pay scales equitable? How many women in your work force must work two jobs? Many women feel forced to choose between raising a family and career advancement. What family policies do you offer? Are most of the women in your office employed in "traditional" female jobs such as secretarial, data entry, or sales clerk? What kind of sexual harassment policy do you have? How clearly is it stated and how easily is it accessed?
- **Ethnic Minorities.** Do you count the numbers of minorities working for you? Which is more important to you, their ethnicity or their productivity? How even-handed are your evaluations of minorities compared with those of white workers?
- **Older Workers.** How comprehensive is your health coverage? Are workers in your office being overlooked because they're old? Do you ever force workers into early retirement?
- **Young Workers.** They may espouse unconventional values and work

styles. They may reject authoritarian management, demand more expla-
nation, and take a more pragmatic approach to solutions. How tolerant
are you of these qualities?

Eliminate Cultural Clashes

Conflict usually arises because of reluctance to discuss issues of cultural
differences. Try to examine routine encounters, foster open dialogue between employees, and identify assumptions they make that can lead to
conflict.

Root Out Institutional Bias

Keep a log for a week, writing down anything you hear or observe that
suggests an intolerance for diversity. Listen to people's vocabularies, especially slang or jargon. Tell-tale warning signs include ignoring cultural
holidays, such as Rosh Hashanah and Martin Luther King, Jr. Day, con-
formist dress codes, an all-female secretarial staff, or offering tickets only
to football games as company perks.

Conduct Diversity Programs

These may be focus groups, retreats, teams of employees meeting on a
regular basis, and language classes. Such programs should be encouraged
and sanctioned by the company and have the sole purpose of promoting
cultural diversity.

Put Someone in Charge of Diversity

You need leaders at every level who organize seminars, create mentoring
programs, and arrange networks. The whole issue of managing diversity
is based on respect for the individual. Companies that celebrate cultural
differences will find that managing diversity is simply an extension of their
core healthy company values. Nowhere are these values more evident than
in the treatment of families.

6. WORK AND FAMILY ARE PARTNERS FOR LIFE

Three qualities distinguish the modern employee: Diverse family and
personal lives, blurred boundaries between work and home life, and a
sizable choice of personal and career paths.

The traditional family has disappeared. Fewer than 10 percent of the population lives in the traditional household headed by one male breadwinner. The concept of family has evolved into an emotional grouping for sharing, mutual support, personal growth, and commitment. Today's families include single mothers, gay parents, unmarried couples, and bachelor dads.

Another change is that many people are taking their work home. Two contributors to this blending of work and family lives are the reverse of the exodus of women from the home to the office, and men's growing attention to the needs of their families.

The linear career with its predictable climb up the corporate ladder is a thing of the past. Today, we are moving along increasingly diverse paths. Consider these statistics: 18 million Americans work part-time; the average age of evening students is 38; people change jobs an average of every three years.

Unfortunately, business has clung to some faulty assumptions:

- **Myth: Family is a women's issue.** The faulty assumption that young mothers should not work and that men are not interested in their families is, fortunately, disappearing quickly and soon will cease to exist. Both men and women should be able to arrange their lives without apology. Managing one's family life is a priority for *both* men and women in the work force.

- **Myth: There is no such thing as a balanced life.** A workaholic may do more damage than good to your company. Know the signs of workaholism: fear of failure, low tolerance for mistakes, chronic headaches or ulcers, and excessive drinking or eating.

Creating a Pro-Worker Atmosphere

Personal concerns are tested with the same seriousness as work concerns in a healthy company. Understanding specific needs throughout the life cycle can help a company respond to these needs:

- **Ages 20 to 30.** People in this young age group are under tremendous pressure to start a career. They may try to conform and imitate, rather than develop personal styles.

- **Ages 31 to 40.** These are the years when employees are often pulled in many directions. Their children are beginning school, women may be returning to work, and aging parents may need assistance. The healthy company must be sensitive to family pressures.

- **Ages 41 to 50.** This is a period of great gains and great losses. Many employees in this age range need time for thoughtful evaluation of career, accomplishments, and families.

- **Ages 51 to 60.** Most people begin to slow down during this period. They acquire a sense of realism about work and personal dreams. At the same time, they may continue to charge forward. Flexibility is important for this group.

- **Age 60 and Up.** Remember that people in this age group may still be active contributors to both career and family. As the median age of the American population climbs, it is a mistake to write off our older workers.

Enhancing the Individual

Here are some ways healthy companies respond to the importance of personal and family life.

Establish Flexible Time

Variable schedules, or flextime, are becoming the norm. The key to success is to establish a clear contract between employer and employee. What does the employer need to have done, and how can a rotating, flexible shift meet those needs? It's important to have core hours when all employees are at work. Some employees may want mornings free, others may want afternoons. Equitable scheduling is important.

Offer Job Sharing

In job sharing, two people split one full-time job, taking on related, but separate assignments. This works best with stressful jobs, where two heads are better than one (but the two heads must be able to communicate!).

Allow Employees to Work at Home

Working at home allows employees to manage their family lives. It can also boost their morale *and* their productivity. The best off-site employees require little supervision and are highly motivated.

Sponsor Sabbaticals

These long leaves of absence help employees sort out personal concerns, recharge batteries, and renew loyalty to employers.

The Family-Friendly Company

Behind these programs are the values of a family-friendly company. Here are nine steps to help you instill these values in your company:

- **Develop a Corporate Family Policy.** Officially note the importance of family values in policy statements.

- **Create a Work-Family Task Force.** The members of this task force should represent a wide variety of your employees.

- **Appoint a Manager for Family Affairs.** This person ensures that family-friendly rhetoric is put into action.

- **Educate Employees on How to be Family-Friendly.** Parenting seminars and referral services are examples of how companies help educate their employees about their options.

- **Design Benefits for All Ages.** Determine that all employees have sufficient coverage.

- **Expand Family Leave.** Include maternity leave, paternity leave, and death-in-the-family leave under one umbrella.

- **Offer Assistance for Employee Dependents.** Child care is becoming an essential benefit for the healthy company.

- **Manage Relocation the Right Way.** Companies that ignore family traumas associated with moving will end up with unhappy employees.

- **Cater to Older Workers.** They are the answer to the growing labor shortages in America.

Creating a family-friendly workplace is just one part of the healthy family. As we move into the 21st century, American business must take the lead in adopting values that honor and respect every individual.

AS THE FUTURE BECOMES THE PRESENT

What will the most admired company in America look like in the year 2000? As a leader and an entrepreneur, you will help control its direction. Look closely and you will see the beginnings of a movement in which a growing number of American businesses are adopting family-friendly, socially conscious values. Some of the companies who have already done this include large companies such as Motorola, Corning, Levi Strauss, and Herman Miller, and small companies such as Hanna Andersson Children's Clothing and Stonyfield Yogurt. Their success is measured by their customers, employees, shareholders, and the communities they serve. They are living proof that businesses based on healthy values not only survive—they thrive.

These companies are unique because of their uncompromising commitment to humanistic values, trusting relationships with learning-oriented employees, long-term relationships with customers, risk-taking, and partnerships with their communities and the environment.

It is the great entrepreneurial challenge of our time to create new organizations that espouse these values. The only people who can build these healthy companies are those who live by these values themselves and who have the vision to create a world in which these values flourish.

BIBLIOGRAPHY

Bennis, W. *On Becoming a Leader.* Reading, Mass.: Addison-Wesley, 1989.

Cataldo, M. F., and T. J. Coates, eds. *Health and Industry: A Behavioral Perspective.* New York: John Wiley, 1986.

Friedman, D., and W. Gray. *A Life Cycle Approach to Family Benefits and Policies.* New York: The Conference Board, 1989.

Kanter, R. M. *When Giants Learn to Dance.* New York: Simon & Schuster, 1989.

Kravetz, D. J. *The Human Resource Revolution.* San Francisco: Jossey-Bass, 1988.

Rosen, Robert. *The Healthy Company: Eight Strategies to Overlap People, Productivity, & Profits.* New York: Putnam Publishing Co., 1991.

Schein, E., ed. *The Art of Managing Human Resources.* New York: Oxford University Press, 1987.

8

Seven Keys to Shaping the Entrepreneurial Organization

Michie P. Slaughter

Many businesses are similar with respect to products, services, and markets. Yet some seem to grow rapidly, passing through higher and higher levels of complexity in the firm while others do not achieve significant growth. For the growth-oriented firms, barriers to transitions that the firm must overcome in the pursuit of growth appear to be only minor disturbances. When this occurs, it is not the result of action of the "lone ranger" entrepreneur, but the action of a purpose-driven team and organization that is committed to the goals and directions established for the firm. When this purpose-driven attitude or entrepreneurial spirit has been established, the transition from entrepreneurial leader to entrepreneurial organization has been achieved. The entrepreneurial organization may look like any other firm. Yet it thrives on an attitude toward growth that exists only when a team spirit is fostered among the associates and with the suppliers and customers of the firm.

Shaping the entrepreneurial organization is not a difficult process when growth, strongly supported by the founders and the top management team, is well planned and constantly reinforced. When these conditions exist, a seven-step approach can be used to implement the process and achieve the desired results.

These seven steps are: 1) hire self-motivated people; 2) help others be successful; 3) create clarity in the organization—clarification of purpose, direction, structure, and measurement; 4) determine and communicate your own values and philosophies; 5) provide appropriate reward systems; 6) create an experimental learning attitude; and 7) celebrate your victories.

The key to the success of most growing organizations is that the entrepreneur has put together a team of highly qualified people who are committed to the goals and objectives of the firm. This does not minimize the importance of identifying opportunities in the marketplace, and developing products or services that satisfy the opportunity or need while producing a profit. Nor does it mean that the judicious use of resources to achieve growth is not a necessary criterion for success. What it does mean is that the successful entrepreneur has expanded his or her capabilities by delegating responsibilities for various functions to a team of motivated people who share the goals and objectives of the entrepreneur leading the firm.

The successful entrepreneurs we read about in the national press are not "Lone Rangers" who have accomplished their greatness through individual achievement. Rather, they are skilled, motivated individuals with a dream who have been able to gather around them similarly skilled people who share their dreams and help make them come true! The ability to build an entrepreneurial organization is, therefore, essential to entrepreneurial success.

Fortunately, many successful entrepreneurs are willing to share the secrets of building effective, entrepreneurial organizations. I have had the good fortune to be associated with a number of these "master" entrepreneurs and have learned many of their secrets. Most notable among this list of masters were two who served as mentors and teachers to me while, together, we built several successful entrepreneurial teams.

In 1950, Ewing Marion Kauffman founded Marion Laboratories, Inc. in the basement of his home in Kansas City. By the time of his death in 1993, "Mr. K," as he was known throughout the Midwest, had built Marion into a company of 3,400 dedicated people with $1 billion dollars in sales and valued at more than $6 billion dollars on the New York Stock Exchange. When the company merged with the Merrell Dow arm of Dow Chemical in 1989, more than 300 of his "associates" became millionaires as a result of his unique philosophy of sharing with those who produced the dramatic growth and profitability of the company.

Gerald W. Holder retired as senior vice president and chief adminis-trative officer of Marion Laboratories in 1985. He had joined Mr. K in 1973 to help him build an executive team capable of doing $100 million in business. At that time, the company had sales of just over $50 million. Prior to 1973, Mr. Holder had enjoyed a successful career building growth-creating organizations for pharmaceutical and chemical firms such as Abbott and Union Carbide. At the time of his death in 1992, Mr. Holder was still teaching entrepreneurs how to build the capacity for growth into their companies.

Much of what I have learned about building entrepreneurial organiza-tions came at the elbows of these two great men or through exposure to other teachers they enabled me to meet. Our goal now at the Center for Entrepreneurial Leadership is to find effective ways to teach the entre-preneurial skills learned from these and other successful entrepreneurs to emerging entrepreneurs so that they might continue the legacy of eco-nomic vitality that is so essential to the growth of our nation. This chapter is an abbreviated version of the seven keys to building entrepreneurial organizations. While you may recognize some of these keys as practical applications of organization research you have read about in the past, oth-ers will strike you as an "obvious" practical application of what we know about human nature to building entrepreneurial teams.

Several books have been written on this topic, some of which are in-cluded in the bibliography. But there is no substitute for experience and the information we learn from our mentors.

These seven keys are by no means the only things you need to do in building entrepreneurial success, but they will give you a head start in understanding the ingredients necessary to build an effective entrepreneu-rial team.

HIRE SELF-MOTIVATED PEOPLE

Anyone who is a sports fan understands that the key to winning is having a talented, motivated team. But in business, we too often settle for talent that's "just good enough," talent we feel we can afford. When we do that, we compromise what our company can become. Entrepreneurs need to hire the very best people they can find—people who bring their motivation with them. In addition to people with great technical skills, you need people who will share your dream with you and work with you to make it become reality. This means you need people with inner drive who give off energy of their own. Avoid people who constantly need to be motivated by you or others.

People who can motivate others have an ability to draw on those who are already strongly motivated from within. They will work hard to find ways to tap into that motivation and avoid actions that turn it off. When trying to build a solid business, most of us don't have the time or skills to create motivation in others where it doesn't already exist, so we need to structure our selection process to find those who are self-motivated. The most effective way to do this is to learn what has been the source of a candidate's motivation in the past. Since past behavior is still the most reliable predictor of future behavior, we can learn about this directly from the candidate by asking "why" he or she did certain things in their lives. You often have to probe to understand real reasons for an action, but by doing so you will gain insight into how they think and what things guided them in making key decisions in their lives. In each case, you will be looking for signs that tell you whether these people look inside for the energy, drive, and direction in their lives, or look to others for these elements. As entrepreneurs, we need people who can guide themselves.

In addition to asking the candidate why he or she took certain actions, you can learn more about how the person actually behaves by asking for real life examples of how they have handled certain situations in the past. For example, ask for a specific example of how the candidate responded to a major setback ("What was the setback and how did you deal with it?") rather than posing a hypothetical question such as "How would you deal with a setback?" This requires the candidate to speak from experience and gives you some past behavior to evaluate. You can then use the example as a window into the person's motivation by asking the follow-up question, "Why did you choose that course of action?"

Remember, each of us puts our best foot forward in interview situations. To get the most information from an interview, we must probe for details and examples. You can then confirm these examples and the candidate's version of them when you call the references the candidate has given you. Having real examples to discuss with the reference will get you past the tendency to obtain only dates of employment and job titles, limited information which has become the norm in today's litigious society.

Ewing Kauffman offered his own personal twist to the talent equation with the advice to entrepreneurs to "Hire people who are smarter than you! In doing so, you prevent limiting the organization to the level of your own ability . . . and you grow the capabilities of your company." Kauffman said, "Someone has to be the smartest guy in the room. Never invest in that man! Put your bets on those who hire the best and smartest people they can find." He further explained, "If you hire people you consider smarter than you, you are more likely to listen to their thoughts and ideas, and this is the best way to expand on your own capabilities and build the strength of your company."

HELP EACH OTHER BE SUCCESSFUL

To build Marion Laboratories, Ewing Kauffman worked hard to create ways his associates could realize their own dreams by helping him realize the dreams he had for the company. His "treat others as you would be treated" philosophy and belief that "those who produce should share in the profits" are excellent examples of establishing the climate for such a partnership mentality. MacGregor (1985) referred to this as an "integration of individual and organizational goals." In the South, it is often referred to as "the way folks are." An old Southern saw says, "Given the opportunity, people will tend to act in their own best interest. . . . Not given the opportunity, people will still tend to act in their own best interest." Clearly one good way to build a successful organization is to find ways to have your own interests be in concert with those you employ.

If you want a "we're all in this together" mentality, you must create one! To do so, you must find out the goals, dreams, and aspirations of your people. This means taking the time to ask and listen. This becomes more difficult as the organization grows in size, but if you establish the concept early in the process, supervisors and managers will sustain it as the company grows. Indeed, it is essential that you encourage the management team to follow this practice. Only by requiring them to do so can you demonstrate your own commitment to the principle. People often watch how we treat others (and how we allow them to treat others) as true signs of how we will treat them!

This process will help you learn what is important to those who will determine your success. For some, the motivator will be money; for others, it will be recognition, achievement, growth, freedom, and autonomy, or even time to be with their children. The important thing to remember is that motivations vary greatly from person to person. The key is to find out what motivates the person you want to motivate.

Responding to the interests and dreams of your people requires that you treat them as distinct and separate individuals. This flies in the face of the cliché that "the only way to be fair is to treat everyone the same." We have all experienced examples of the illogical behavior required when an organization "treats everybody the same." Responding to individual needs will make it possible to create conditions in which individuals' dreams will mesh with yours.

CREATE CLARITY IN THE ORGANIZATION— CLARITY OF PURPOSE, DIRECTION, STRUCTURE, AND MEASUREMENT

In his analysis of the successful growth of Marion Laboratories, Gerald W. Holder attributed much of the organization's strength to an entrepreneurial leadership team that focused significant energy on creating clarity throughout the work force. This enabled people to operate with a commonality of understanding and the assurance that everyone was working together. Holder believed strongly that creating clarity in the organization was the most important role for leadership. It required that leaders first establish clarity for themselves, then implement a major communications and reinforcement effort to create it for the organization. He acknowledged that complete clarity is never attained in a growing organization; however, the changes that come with growth only increase the importance of clear thinking and clear communications. Following are the four clarities Holder identified as critical to the success of Marion Laboratories.

Clarity of Purpose

It is important that people know why the organization exists. People need a reason to give you their enthusiastic support. Do not expect anyone but your family (and often not even them) to get excited about "making you rich." Most people will not mind if you make lots of money if they share in the gain with you. But most still need a purpose that is grander than money. Becoming the first or becoming the best or even doing what no one else has ever done in a given business or industry are challenges which excite people. Helping people solve problems or lead better, safer, healthier, and more productive lives are the kinds of things that call upon the best of human values and stir people to committed action. Since no product or service will survive unless it meets a true need in the market-place, the opportunity to meet that need better, more quickly, or less expensively often provides the real purpose for an organization.

The people with entrepreneurial spirit who you want in your company will enjoy the opportunity to build and create a business where none has existed before. Give them the opportunity to share in the excitement of this building process by communicating why you are willing to make your own personal sacrifice to make it happen. If after deep personal reflection your only reason is to "get rich," reconsider the whole thing. Your cus-tomers, employees, suppliers, and investors will want you to have a purpose beyond personal wealth before they will share the risk with you. You must realize that each of them must share your risk in order for you to succeed.

Clarity of Direction

Without careful thought and communication, people often wonder "Where are we headed with this business?" or "What kinds of skills and talent do we need to bring into the company?" This does not mean that the direction is set in concrete and is unchangeable; rather, it means that the current direction often results in the diffusion of scarce resources in areas of minimal or even counterproductive return.

Clarity of Structure

The next key challenge in a growing business is the coordination of "Who's going to do what?" and "What part of the job is mine and what is yours?" and "Whose responsibility is it?" When you are the sole em-ployee, this is not a problem. But when the company begins to grow beyond what you can do alone, it becomes a consuming task of leadership. I am not referring to the dreaded organizational chart here, but rather to the process of thinking through and communicating to your team the roles, responsibilities, and accountabilities of each so they can devote their efforts fully and confidently to doing their part.

We all watch with admiration when a shortstop and second baseman turn a double play, when an alley-oop pass results in a slam dunk basket, or when a trap block springs a runner free for a touchdown. The same level of knowledge, forethought, planning, and practice are required in the entrepreneurial firm in creating, recognizing, and capitalizing on opportunities. In each sports case cited above, the players must know and have confidence in the roles and responsibilities of their teammates, in addition to their own roles and responsibilities. This knowledge and confidence allows them to concentrate on their own job and give it their full energy while recognizing the interdependence of the players. No less is necessary for the growing firm. Deciding who will do what is sometimes difficult. But *not* deciding will always create difficulty. The entrepreneur must stay alert to the evolutionary changes in the organization that can bring about confusion related to who is to do what and work to keep it clear.

Clarity of Measurement

Knowing how to measure the results in a business is as essential as knowing how to score in an athletic event. Too often, though, we assume that everyone understands and fail to make it clear. Sometimes even the entrepreneur misunderstands how the customer or the investor will measure performance and is surprised when one or both withdraw their support. As businesses become increasingly complex, it becomes more difficult to determine what the key measures of success are. In many cases, there is a significant time lag between initial action and the end result. Careful thought to interim milestones in the development of the business is essential to making changes in direction, allocation of resources, rewarding people, and a variety of critical decisions the entrepreneur must make. Americans are great "measurers." We equate changes in measurements with achievement. We have more statistics on every aspect of both individual and team performance in sports such as baseball and basketball than the inventors of the games ever imagined, but we often overlook the importance of similar measurements in our business. Since people often pay more attention to the things they know you are going to measure, it is important that you make sure you are measuring the things that you have decided are important to you. Your people should have access to the information that will allow them to measure these things, too. If these things are sensitive financial information and you are reluctant to share it, consider how long you would exert your energy in a game, such as bowling, where you couldn't keep score and didn't know how well you were doing or if someone else was keeping score and wouldn't tell you how you were doing. If you still have that reluctance, please read Jack Stack's book, *The Great Game of Business,* which describes how he used open-book management to turn a dying business into an exciting entrepreneurial venture.

DETERMINE AND COMMUNICATE YOUR OWN VALUES AND PHILOSOPHIES

The importance of values and philosophy has received a great deal of attention during the last few years. Much of that attention, however, has been focused on the quality of the values and their goodness, or lack thereof. While very important, the quality of the values is not enough. Your values must be clearly communicated and consistent with your actions to have a positive impact on your business. They must be reinforced by both your words and your actions. Ewing Kauffman's philosophies of "treat others as you would be treated" and "those who produce should share in the results" would have had little impact on his business had he not constantly expressed them in both word and deed.

Values and philosophies are also important in providing a basis for making decisions and a basis for teaching people in the organization how to make decisions. Clearly stated, consistent values provide a framework within which people can make the myriad of major and minor decisions required daily in their jobs. Large bureaucratic organizations try to communicate direction through often complicated and voluminous policies and procedures, sometimes presented in multiple volumes of three-ring binders. Creating such manuals requires an impossible ability to know in advance all circumstances in any situation, or the result is illogical action "just because that's our policy!"

A clearly communicated set of values allows people at various levels in an organization to know what is important to the leadership and how those leaders would go about making a decision. Understanding the stated values helps people make decisions appropriate to the organization and its leaders. The internalization of values can help expand capacity, because that understanding clears the way for delegating more decisions to others. Since associates will often have more current and complete information than the leader, such delegation can reduce your risk while expanding your capacity. Every entrepreneur knows that reducing risk while expanding capacity is as elusive as cold fusion. Achieving clarity of values is a very effective way to do just that.

PROVIDE APPROPRIATE REWARD SYSTEMS

Most entrepreneurs think of "rewards" in the narrow context of compensation, namely bonus plans. There is great power, however, in a broader interpretation of the term. Effective reward systems include all forms of compensation, plus the wide variety of other things that are important to people in a work setting, such as job assignment, recognition, growth and learning, additional responsibility, authority, and autonomy. Mr. Kauffman was a firm believer in the simple, but powerful concept of appreciation as a reward and motivator. The effectiveness of any reward system is a function of two primary factors: whether or not the recipient perceives the reward as a positive, and whether the reward actually encourages the desired behavior. A third factor, judicious use, preserves the value of a reward and recognizes that any reward given indiscriminately loses value quickly.

Our assumption that something we would consider a reward would be viewed in the same way by an associate often results in the use of rewards that disappoint. Some rewards actually represent punishment to the recipient. For example, early in my career I once received an award for having done an outstanding job leading a fund raising campaign, a project which I found to be an unpleasant experience. The reward was being named to head the campaign again the following year. It is no surprise that the best way to find out what an associate values as reward is to ASK!

In order for the reward to be effective, it must encourage the desired behavior, and the desired behavior must be consistent with the strategy you have designed for your business. I have often seen sales bonuses used as rewards for opening new accounts, at the same time a key element in the marketing strategy is maintaining and servicing current accounts. In one case, the sales bonus plan actually took off points for time spent prospecting new accounts when "growing the customer base" was an essential part of the company strategy. The key here, of course, is that there is no right or wrong. Just be sure you are rewarding the behavior you really want. Ideally, people should be able to look at their pay and other rewards to learn the keys to good performance. It is the leader's responsibility to make sure the reward system is set up to support the business strategy.

CREATE AN EXPERIMENTAL, LEARNING ATTITUDE

One of the biggest failings of our education system at every level is the process of teaching that there is always ONE right answer (and it's in the back of the book!). In most entrepreneurial settings, it is clear that, "No one has ever done what you have set out to do!" In almost every case, there will be several good ways—some will be better than others and some will be truly untried. The wise entrepreneur will take advantage of this dynamic and encourage associates to experiment, to look for and try different ways to do a task better, to come up with novel solutions. Acknowledging that you don't know all of the answers yourself can free up your team to help find solutions, and it presents an opportunity for them to contribute to your success. An enthusiastic, "we're making this up as we go along" attitude can do wonders to keep people looking for better ways to improve your product or service.

In these days of continuous improvement, it is critical to establish an experimental attitude to create the freedom to try new things. Such an attitude also sets the stage for change when an experiment doesn't work out. Rather than spending great energy trying to prove you are right, you can more easily say, "That's not working, let's try another way!" Or as Stevenson (1985) said, "The best entrepreneurs are the ones who 'fail quickly' and get on with learning how to do it better." Establishing an "experimental, learning attitude" can turn early failures into success.

CELEBRATE YOUR VICTORIES!

Good people want to be associated with a winner! We see sports fans in cities large and small engage in totally irrational behavior just to establish their affiliation with a winning team. Yet we often fail to give our associates an opportunity to celebrate their association with the victories we enjoy in our business. We see kids and adults give each other "high five's" when they get a hit, sink a putt, or make a touchdown. Why not when you make a big sale, secure that new account, or get that "nice job" from an important customer? Simple, spontaneous joy can be great motivational fuel for that next challenge.

BIBLIOGRAPHY

Holder, G.W., and Kenneth McKensie. *A Theory of Marion.* Marion: Laboratory
  Internal Publication, 1986.

MacGregor, Douglas. *The Human Side of Enterprise.* New York: McGraw Hill,
  1985.

Mintzburg, H. *Power in and Around Organizations.* Englewood Cliffs, N.J.: Prentice-Hall, 1983.

Pascarella, P., and M. A. Frohman. *The Purpose Driven Organization.* San Francisco: Josey-Bass, 1989.

Rosen, Robert H. *The Healthy Company.* New York: Putnam Publishing Co.,
  1991.

Stack, John P. *The Great Game of Business.* New York: Currency Books, 1992.

Stevenson, Howard, and D. E. Gumpert. "The Heart of Entrepreneurship," *Harvard Business Review* 63, no. 2 (1985): 85–94.

Part III

Multidimension: Building Valuable Companies

9

Making the Entrepreneurial Team Work

Lee G. Bolman and Terrence E. Deal

The world is changing and entrepreneurs must change with it. They must think global instead of local; focus on psychic needs rather than material needs; develop decentralized and democratic organizations; and adapt to a multicultural and multivocal world. Leadership must be by and for everyone in their organization. Leadership in the 1990s must be understood as relationship and mutual influence instead of individual heroism and unilateral exercise of power.

Microsoft's competition with IBM and the development of Microsoft's Windows NT to compete with IBM's OS/2 is a case study in how new leadership skills can work. How Microsoft structured its development teams, attended to the teams' human needs, handled the political components of teamwork, and instilled the teams with vision, soul, and magic help account for the company's successful development of its new software package. Each member of a team must feel commitment and passion from the entrepreneurial leader. They must have clear focus, structure, and high performance expectations. They must feel a sense of ownership, contribution, and achievement.

The world we live in is changing very fast. These changes pose challenges that entrepreneurs, like other organizational leaders, are finding more and more difficult to solve. Most are part of a larger set of forces that have been brewing for the last two centuries and show no signs of abating in the foreseeable future. To provide the leadership that society needs in the years ahead, entrepreneurs and other leaders must dramatically transform their style.

Before change can happen, entrepreneurs must answer three difficult questions:

1. What kind of leadership does my organization need?
2. What kind of leadership is it getting?
3. If there is a gap, how do I respond to it?

Ideas about leadership change slowly because they are deeply rooted in remarkably stable cultural values and beliefs. As Serieyx (1993, 15) commented, "The organizations of yesterday are today's mental prison. They keep us from seeing the new ways to lead and manage that tomorrow's world demands and today's changes make possible. . . . To escape our mental prisons, we have to take hold of the keys that today's changes offer us. To speed the process, we have to free ourselves of our own outmoded ideas."

FOUR LEADERSHIP FRAMES

To understand kinds of leadership, four distinctive leadership frames or lenses have been identified.

The first, the structural frame, emphasizes rationality, efficiency, planning, and policies. Structural leaders value analysis and data, keep their eyes on the bottom line, set clear directions, and hold people accountable for results. They try to solve organizational problems by developing new policies and procedures, or by restructuring.

The second, the human resource frame, focuses on the interaction between individual and organizational needs. Human resource leaders value relationships and feelings and seek to lead by using facilitation and empowerment. When problems arise, they are likely to favor remedies like participation and training.

The third lens is the political frame. Political leaders are advocates and negotiators who spend much of their time networking, creating coalitions, building a power base, and brokering compromises. They see conflict as a source of energy rather than a cause for alarm.

Finally, the symbolic frame sees a chaotic world in which meaning and predictability are socially constructed. In this frame, facts are social interpretations rather than concrete realities. Symbolic leaders pay diligent attention to myth, ritual, ceremony, stories, and other symbolic forms. When things go wrong, they create a new story or revisit cherished values.

All four frames are important because each defines a critical aspect of organizational reality. The four frames can bring into focus the changes taking place in every type of human institution, from families and small groups to multinational corporations and nation states. They are creating a demand for new forms of leadership.

KEY CHANGES IN ORGANIZATIONS AND LEADERSHIP STYLES

Table 9.1 presents a set of hypotheses about the ways organizations are changing, along with the implications of those changes for leadership.

From Local and Simple to Global and Complex

Although the family farm is the archetype of a simple and local production system, the percentage of the U.S. population now living on farms is minuscule, and most farm workers now commute to work just like their urban counterparts. An autocratic, often patriarchal approach was a viable form of leadership on a family farm, where one person could understand most of the important issues, keep track of the essential information, and make most of the key decisions. Consider that form of leadership, and then think about Lou Gerstner, who took over as CEO of IBM in early 1993. As an outsider, Gerstner was confronted with simply trying to make sense out of the many products, technologies, markets, people, and systems that constitute one of the world's largest and most complex organizations. No one person could possibly understand it all. He had to be a good analyst who, with the help of others, could find some order in chaos. He also

TABLE 9.1

Trends in Human Institutions

Dimension of Change	Changes in Systems	Changes in Conception of Leadership
Structural/Technological	From local and simple to global and complex	From autocrat to analyst and social architect
Human	From focus on material needs (e.g., food and shelter) to psychic needs (e.g., lifestyle)	From good father to catalyst and servant
Political	From centralized and authoritarian to decentralized and democratic	From great warrior to negotiator and advocate
Cultural/Symbolic	From monocultural and univocal to multicultural and multivocal	From hero as destroyer of demons to hero as creator of possibilities

Adapted from Bolman and Deal, 1993

needed to be a good architect who could design systems and processes for moving his organization forward. Everyone agreed that more centralization was the last thing IBM needed to reverse its declining fortunes. Gerstner "reengineered" IBM by redesigning its basic structure.

From a Focus on Material Needs to a Focus on Psychic Needs

Forty years ago Maslow proposed his famous hierarchical conception of needs, stating that as humans satisfy more basic physiological needs, they move on to higher, more abstract needs. His work tells us something important about leadership: When subsistence is uncertain, people focus on the basics of food and shelter, and no one has the time, resources, or inclination to satisfy their "abstract" needs. In a subsistence economy, people will accept the authority of a benevolent father figure who can assure them of a basic standard of living. But in places where a substantial part of the population is well off, as in the United States and much of Western Europe, the general store is replaced by countless different boutiques, each focused on the lifestyle interests of a particular market segment. An affluent middle class expects its leaders to be democratic and to be responsive to people's needs and desires.

From Centralized and Authoritarian to Decentralized and Democratic

Historically, governments have been centralized and authoritarian, headed by an absolute monarch or select aristocracy. As recently as the middle of this century, most of the world's population lived under governments that were autocratic or totalitarian. Many of these systems have failed. The collapse of the planned economy in the Soviet Union and the retreat from central planning in China are two of the more dramatic examples. In a centralized system, the leader was the warrior who could lead the organization to victory against its enemies. In a diverse, global village, such a leader is counterproductive. Instead, what is needed are leaders who are not only strong, but who are wise and flexible enough to effectively negotiate with all the other players on what is a very complex political field.

From Monocultural and Univocal to Multicultural and Multivocal

When few people traveled outside their own national and cultural boundaries, systems at every level were usually monocultural and univocal, dominated by one culture's values. Today, the proliferation of such technologies as jet airplanes and fax machines has caused cultures to collide and to interpenetrate one another. Music, art, movies, technologies, products, and tourists cross national and cultural boundaries at a dizzying pace. The resulting collisions and miscommunications are often painful and frustrating. Managers find themselves surrounded by disparate groups with divergent values, each of whom has a variety of demands.

It is no longer possible in multicultural societies such as the United States or the former Soviet Union for a single cultural voice to dominate the national conversation. One of the contradictions of our time, as Serieyx (1993, 26) said, is the risk that "the globalization of problems leads to the balkanization of values, the retreat into self, the exclusion of others and social disintegration."

The same economic and technological developments that make the global village possible also undermine centralized, univocal systems because authority is pushed aside and multiple parties become involved in decision making. Disparate voices insist on being heard, and the effectiveness of the leadership depends on its ability to capitalize on the advantages of diversity—while minimizing its costs. Such a world can ill afford the old image of the hero who goes forth to slay whatever evil force is besetting the village or the nation. Leaders who view outsiders as the enemy promote ethnic hatred and produce the devastating cultural conflict that we have seen in Bosnia, the Middle East, and elsewhere. Today's leaders must strive for mutual learning and appreciation. They must seek ways to work constructively and collaboratively within their nation's cultural boundaries.

SHIFTS IN HOW WE THINK ABOUT LEADERSHIP

Embedded in these changes in leadership style are two fundamental shifts in how we think about leadership. The first is a change from a belief in leadership by and for the few to leadership by and for the many.

This is a change from the idea that leadership is reserved for a few people in high places, or for those fortunate enough to belong to the right social class, ethnic group, or gender. This shift has occurred for reasons that are both functional and ideological. Functionally, the forms of leadership that worked in an earlier time and place aren't appropriate for late 20th century society. Ideologically, this shift is necessary to rescue leadership from the view that it is indistinguishable from power, and, by extension, from oppression.

The second change is a shift from leadership as individual heroism and unilateral exercise of power to leadership as relationship and mutual influence.

Leadership is often seen as a one-way process: Leaders lead and followers follow. In reality, leaders and followers have a complex relationship and must be studied in tandem. As Cronin said:

> The study of leadership needs inevitably to be linked or merged with the study of followership. We cannot really study leaders in isolation from followers, constituents or group members. The leader is very much a product of the group, and very much shaped by its aspirations, values and human resources. The more we learn about leadership, the more the leader-follower linkage is understood and reaffirmed. A two-way engagement or two-way interaction is constantly going on. When it ceases, leaders become lost, out of touch, imperial, or worse. (Cronin 1984, 24–25)

BUILDING THE ENTREPRENEURIAL TEAM

Bill Gates was in the right place at the right time in the early 1980s when IBM's fledgling personal computer needed an operating system. The result was DOS, the product of a David and Goliath collaboration that is now the operating system for most of the world's personal computers. It helped Microsoft become the world's largest software firm and started founder and CEO Bill Gates on the road to becoming one of the richest men in America. Windows, a graphic interface that rides atop DOS, fueled another great leap forward for Gates' Microsoft empire.

But by the late 1980s, the handwriting was on the wall: DOS would soon be obsolete, woefully deficient for existing PCs and totally inadequate for future technology. For a period of time, it looked as if the new operating system would be OS/2, jointly developed by Microsoft and IBM. But what had once been a happy and productive partnership began to

TABLE 9.2

Making the Entrepreneurial Team Work

Dimension of Group Process	Key Issues
Structural/Technological	Clear focus, appropriate structure High performance expectations
Human	Ownership Contribution Achievement
Political	Cultivate conflict Balance of power
Cultural/Symbolic	Compelling vision Soul and magic

dissolve, and when Microsoft and IBM finally parted company, IBM took OS/2 with it.

Microsoft's future depended on beating IBM (and several other companies) across the finish line in developing the next great operating system for PCs. What was needed was a system that could handle the dramatic increases in speed, memory, and complexity of existing and future generations of personal computers, while still running everything ever written for DOS or Windows. It took five years and a team of 200 software developers before Microsoft had its answer: Windows NT.

The behind-the-scenes story of the development of Windows by entrepreneur Bill Gates, and an entrepreneur, David Cutler, who was hired by Gates, illustrates many of the key issues every entrepreneur faces in building a cohesive, committed, high-performing creative team. The Windows NT story demonstrates how savvy, risk-taking entrepreneurial leaders can use those issues to their advantage. Table 9.2 lists the dimensions of change that are part of these issues.

Gates went outside Microsoft to recruit Cutler, a former executive at Digital Equipment Corporation (DEC). At DEC, Cutler had led the team that wrote VMS, the operating system that played a key role in Digital's domination of the mini-computer industry (Zachary 1993). *The Wall Street Journal* described Cutler as a rough-cut combination of Captain Bligh and Captain Ahab. Even Gates agreed that Cutler was known "more for his code than his charm" (Zachary 1993, A-1). Gates himself is not known for his humility. Industry insiders agree that he is brilliant, and variously describe him as focused, driven, and ruthless. He had created a culture at Microsoft that thrived on confrontation, and someone with Cutler's brash reputation seemed just the man for the next mission.

Structuring the Team

Teams rarely succeed if their focus is murky or incoherent. Cutler had clear focus from the start. He needed to develop an ambitious new operating system. His team's biggest challenge was not so much to figure out what to do, but to figure out how to do it.

A clear focus is of little help unless a team's structure fits its task. Cutler initially divided the Windows NT team into three groups, each with specific responsibilities. The three groups were subdivided into five to ten work groups, some as small as three to four people, and each with responsibility for a basic segment of the program.

While this decentralized structure enabled each team to be highly specialized, it created substantial coordination problems. How do you ensure that all the pieces created by each component would fit together into a coherent whole? Cutler addressed this problem by holding daily meetings and, particularly, by insisting on a daily "build." Every day, a testing team tested the entire system-in-process on dozens of different computers in an effort to find all the bugs. It was an exacting and stressful approach to coordination. Cutler's demanding presence added even more stress:

> Cutler blasts through the door leading to Microsoft's Build Lab. He is not happy. It is 10:20 Monday morning, May 3, and the daily "build" of the program, called Windows NT, is not finished yet. As a leader of the NT team, Mr. Cutler insists that a new build, or test version, of NT be stitched together electronically each morning so that his programmers can, as he puts it, "eat their own dog food." Mr. Cutler is angry about the delay, angry about a botched test the day before, angry at the world. After glaring at a computer screen, he storms out of the lab, leaving a distinct chill. Two

builders, Kyle Shannon and Arden White, dip into a king-size jar of Ro-laids, popping one each. The day has soured early. (Zachary 1993, 1)

The daily build provided immediate feedback and made public every programming error. Combined with Cutler's demands for perfection, this approach was a logical and powerful way to link different part of the program together, while encouraging each group to set very high perform-ance standards.

The Human Side of Effective Teams

Several decades of research (Bolman and Deal 1991; Hackman and Oldham 1980; Hackman et al. 1990) suggest that, more than anything else, members of high-performing teams are motivated by a sense of own-ership, contribution, and achievement. They feel responsibility for their own work, they understand how it contributes to a larger whole, and they feel that their efforts and energy will accomplish something worthwhile.

Cutler's strategy made his teams high performing. The overall structure of the Windows NT project was flat and decentralized. Teams were kept small and were basically autonomous, with each having clear responsibility for its own piece of the program. Each also knew how vital its part was to the whole. Because every team received continual feedback about the results of its efforts, team members knew on a daily basis how their con-tribution was assisting or impeding progress on the system. They invested themselves in the process and felt a sense of ownership for what they accomplished.

The Political Side of Team-Building

In any creative or entrepreneurial task requiring contributions from a variety of disciplines or perspectives, conflict is inevitable. While too much conflict can undermine effectiveness, too little can be even worse. The fear of chaos often leads organizations to smother conflict, thereby losing its benefits.

As Heffron (1989, 185) said, "A tranquil, harmonious organization may very well be an apathetic, uncreative, stagnant, inflexible, and unresponsive organization. Conflict challenges the status quo, stimulates interest and curiosity. It is the root of personal and social change, creativity, and innovation. Conflict encourages new ideas and approaches to problems, stimulating innovation."

Cutler firmly believed that conflict was essential to the Windows NT mission, and he deliberately cultivated it, often pitting engineers against each other in a search for solutions. To prevent the resulting cacophony from turning into unproductive and divisive warfare, he drew clear boundaries for acceptable conflict. The basic mission was non-negotiable, but substantive debate about how to get there was solicited and encouraged.

Balancing conflict also requires an appropriate balance of power, avoiding both overcentralization and fragmentation. No one doubted that Cutler was in charge, but people also knew they could fight back. He once lit into Johanne Charon, a 27-year-old French-Canadian programmer, asking her, "Why didn't you file that fix earlier in the day?" She retorted, "I was at karate class, kicking butt." Cutler backed off, saying only, "OK."

The Symbolic Side of Teamwork

Structure, people, and politics are all essential elements of successful entrepreneurial team work. But by themselves they are insufficient because they miss the deeper secrets of how effective teams or groups reach the special state of peak performance. As Visa CEO Dee Hock explained it, "In the field of group endeavor, you will see incredible events in which the group performs far beyond the sum of its individual talents. It happens in the symphony, in the ballet, in the theater, in sports, and equally in business. It is easy to recognize and impossible to define. It is a mystique. It cannot be achieved without immense effort, training, and cooperation, but effort, training and cooperation alone rarely create it" (Schlesinger, Eccles, and Gabarro 1983).

CREATING THE MAGIC

When groups excel far beyond anything that could reasonably be expected, they usually have a compelling vision, soul, and a dose of magic. For Gates and Cutler, developing a compelling vision was relatively easy. Windows NT was to be one of the most powerful and complex pieces of software ever created, running faster and doing more than any operating system before it. It was also crucial to Microsoft's long-range strategy of maintaining its dominant position in the industry. Bill Gate's dream was that it would become the operating system for millions of personal computers around the world.

Soul and magic are more elusive: you can't see or touch them, yet you can feel their presence. Team members "feel the spirit" (Vaill 1982). It adds meaning and value to their work. More and more, organizations are realizing that soul and magic are the wellsprings of high performance. You find them in legendary athletic teams such as the Boston Celtics, whose tradition of "Celtics pride" has helped make them one of the most extraordinary winning teams in professional sports.

A team's soul and magic spring from the commitment and passion displayed by its leader. An army colonel tells the story of a general who was reviewing a regiment on a parade field. The weather was threatening and a canopy had been placed over the podium area where the general was standing. When the rain came pouring down, staff officers all tried to crowd in under the canopy. The general calmly stepped out from under the canopy to be in the rain along with everyone else. "No one who was there that day will ever forget that," said the colonel. "That's the kind of guy you would follow anywhere."

Cutler's people felt that way about him. While he was known for his ferocious temper, "you really don't take Dave's outbursts personally," said Mitchell Duncan, his chief builder. "He's not attacking your character. Dave gets in at 6 a.m. He's there every weekend. He's in the trenches."

Yet another important element used by the Windows NT team was humor, which occasionally helped to defuse some of the tension caused by their chief's outbursts. On Cutler's 50th birthday, the team gave him a framed piece of his own office wall—which he had destroyed in a moment of rage ignited by the failure of a new build to run on his computer.

ASSURANCES OF SUCCESS

Structural, human resource, and political leadership frames all contribute to our understanding of entrepreneurial teams.

Structural views remind us that teams cannot excel without clear focus, a structure aligned to the task, and high performance expectations.

Human resource views remind leaders of the importance of assuring that every member of the entrepreneurial team feels a sense of ownership, contribution, and achievement.

The political perspective tells us that it is important for the leader to cultivate conflict while balancing power between leader and team members.

Each perspective is valid and important; we ignore any of them at our peril. But the signs are everywhere that late 20th century organizations are at a critical juncture because of a crisis of meaning and faith. Managers ask themselves questions like, "How am I supposed to build team spirit when my people feel underpaid, money is tight, turnover is increasing, and some people aren't sure they'll even have a job?" Such questions are important, but they are not the only important questions. By themselves, they can limit managerial imagination and divert attention from deeper issues of faith and purpose.

Managers are inescapably accountable for budgets and bottom lines. They must also respond to individual needs, legal requirements, and economic pressures.

But they can serve a deeper, more powerful, and more durable function when they recognize that team-building at its heart is a spiritual undertaking. It is the creation of a community of believers, united by shared faith and shared culture. It is a search for the spirit within. Peak performance emerges as a team discovers its soul.

BIBLIOGRAPHY

Bolman, L. G., and T. E. Deal. *Reframing Organizations: Artistry, Choice and Leadership*. San Francisco: Jossey-Bass, 1991.

Cronin, T. E. "Thinking and Learning about Leadership," *Presidential Studies Quarterly*, (1984) 22–34.

Gue'henno, J-M. *La Fin de la De'mocratie*. Paris: Flammarion, 1993.

Hackman, J. R., and G. R. Oldham. *Work Redesign*. Reading, Mass.: Addison-Wesley, 1980.

Hackman, J. R., ed. *Groups That Work (and Those That Don't): Creating Conditions for Effective Teamwork*. San Francisco: Jossey-Bass, 1990.

Heffron, F. *Organization Theory and Public Organizations: The Political Connection*. Englewood Cliffs, N.J.: Prentice-Hall, 1989.

Schlesinger, L., R. Eccles, and J. Gabarro. *Managerial Behavior in Organizations*. New York: McGraw-Hill, 1983.

Serieyx, H. *Le Big Bang des Organisations*. Paris: Calmann-Le'vy, 1993.

Vaill, P. B. "The Purposing of High-Performance Systems," *Organizational Dynamics* (Autumn 1982): 23–39.

Zachary, G. P. "Climbing the Peak: Agony and Ecstasy of 200 Code Writers Beget Windows NT," *Wall Street Journal*, May 26, 1993, A1.

10

Building Value into the Entrepreneurial Company

Robert Lawrence Kuhn

Creating value in an entrepreneurial firm is as much art as science. Formulas do not accurately predict the value of a business. Good strategy—strategic thinking, strategic planning, and strategic management—build the value of a business. But most business owners are too busy with day-to-day problems to undertake the steps that would help build their company value.

Building value into the entrepreneurial company requires the perspective of the buyer. Value is in the eyes of the buyer, and buyers are looking not only for recent performance but for future potential. Buyers generally buy businesses as generators of cash. Timing is an important factor, and there must be a perception of organizational stability and opportunity for business expansion. Buyers also look for recession resistance, products that fill niche markets, and companies that respond to demographic and socio-economic trends.

Understanding the market for business sales and mergers can assist an entrepreneur in formulating a corporate strategy and using that strategy to build value. There are also specific steps to preparing businesses for sale: 1) avoid long payback investments; 2) plan for organizational success; 3) alter the company's financial management; 4) resolve big issues; and 5) adjust the product mix.

Owners and managers who have difficulty seeing their companies from the perspective of potential buyers may not understand the critical role strategic management can play in enhancing the value of their company for a merger or acquisition.

While all business owners want to increase the value of their businesses, many fail. Most owners are so focused on the day-to-day problems of keeping a business going that they can't undertake the proactive steps that would help build their company's value.

WHAT IS A VALUABLE COMPANY?

The first step in value building is learning to understand what makes a company valuable. Consider the following examples of recently completed Geneva transactions (Table 10.1).

Table 10.1 proves three mergers and acquisitions truisms:

1. No formula, multiple, or rule of thumb can accurately predict the value of a business.
2. Value is in the eyes of the beholder—the buyer.
3. Buyers buy companies not just for their recent performance, but also for their future potential.

Many factors, some financial and some not, influence the value of a company. There's no other way to explain Company 16, with a $1.4 million loss, selling for $10.3 million! You may point out that it had a book equity of $5.6 million to balance the loss, but if you look at Company 15, you'll see that it had a pre-tax loss AND negative equity—yet the company sold for more than $13 million. The bottom line is that buyers look beyond financials when valuing and buying.

INCREASING VALUES

To further complicate the issue, values are subjective and also dynamic. Table 10.2 shows companies that Geneva valued. Within 3 to 18 months,

TABLE 10.1

Recently Completed Geneva Transactions
($ thousands)

Company	Pre-Tax Income	Net Worth	Sales Price
1	1,577	5,013	12,500
2	2,085	4,032	20,000
3	365	1,511	4,150
4	344	680	5,500
5	50	423	914
6	387	574	6,194
7	869	4,304	4,200
8	3,669	8,000	50,600
9	566	1,844	20,000
10	2,286	(1,062)	11,114
11	730	1,223	5,250
12	1,189	(666)	11,500
13	812	3,615	10,500
14	2,893	6,712	10,200
15	(127)	(485)	13,500
16	(1,406)	5,617	10,313

NOTE: Pre-tax income and net worth figures are per financial statements, before recasting. Sales price figures exclude earnout.

Source:
Geneva Data

TABLE 10.2

Increasing Values ($ millions)

Company	Original Value	Revised Value	Time Elapsed	$ Gain	% Gain
A	7.5	22.0	1.5 years	14.5	193%
B	25.0	39.1	1 year	14.1	56%
C	15.0	27.7	8 months	12.7	84%
D	7.5	10.0	1.5 years	12.5	167%
E	7.0	18.8	1.5 years	11.8	169%
F	16.0	25.7	1 year	9.7	61%
G	3.6	11.8	1.5 years	8.2	229%
H	14.0	22.0	3 months	8.0	57%

Source:
Geneva Data

these companies' values had increased dramatically. In as little as 30 months, values increased as much as $14.5 million!

The companies shown in Table 10.2 have nothing inherently special about them. Most are, in fact, in rather mundane industries. Company A, for example, manufactures steel forgings; company B designs and prints soft goods; and company E is a book manufacturer. Again these are not exactly "hot industries," but these "common" businesses used value-building tactics to dramatically increase their values.

DECREASING VALUES

Unfortunately, as Table 10.3 reveals, not all our clients fared as well.

The companies shown in Table 10.3 are companies that Geneva valued and which relinquished up to 80 percent of their value within six months to two and a half years. Reasons for these declines varied. Company A, as one example, experienced value decline because of a radical change in its market—and the company's consequent reaction to that change. A civil engineering and land surveying firm, it serviced the depressed commercial construction market. Because of increased competition for fewer jobs, company A started "buying" contracts. Profit margins declined from a peak of 21 percent to only 6 percent of sales. As the level of cash flow declined, and the risk resulting from the company's poor performance rose, company A's value suffered.

Each of these companies has an interesting story. They share a common thread in that all of them were unwilling or unable to respond to changes in their companies or markets. Some of them lost key customers; others were negatively affected by changing government regulations; and still others simply lost the competitive battle that entrepreneurs fight every day.

These examples prove one of the basic principles of value: It never stays the same. Whether increasing or decreasing, corporate value is always shifting.

VALUE-BUILDING BASICS

Value-building strategy should be restricted neither to large companies nor to business philosophy. Strategic thinking, strategic planning, and strategic management are crucial for small and midsize firms and for market-driven M&A preparation. Simply stated, good strategy

TABLE 10.3

Declining Values ($ millions)

Company	Original Value	Revised Value	Time Elapsed	$ Loss	% Loss
A	2.5	1.2	2.5 years	1.3	52%
B	1.5	0.3	2 years	1.2	80%
C	2.0	1.0	1.5 years	1.0	50%
D	2.0	1.2	1.0 year	0.8	50%
E	2.5	2.0	2.0 years	0.5	20%
F	3.0	2.5	2.5 years	0.5	17%
G	2.0	1.6	6 months	0.4	20%
H	1.1	0.8	8 months	0.3	27%

Source:
Geneva Data

builds the value of a business, and increases company worth and shareholder wealth. Good value-building strategy focuses on what serious buyers pay for when they purchase businesses—and then seeks to implement those programs. Such a strategy always stresses what will really work.

What kinds of strategies can effectively augment the price that a serious buyer would willingly pay for a company? Such value-building strategies are often not apparent (although sometimes they may be too apparent) and are occasionally quite simple. Sometimes, the elimination of certain impediments to help realize company value can have an enormous impact on price, and yet be easily implemented.

As a general rule, buyers buy businesses as generators of cash; therefore, the greater and more certain the flows of net free cash, the higher the price buyers will pay and the better the deal they will make. The bottom line is that the reward of the cash flow must be weighed against the risk of the uncertainty of obtaining that cash flow. In other words, the value-building task is to grow cash flow, and at the same time project confidence that this will continue to occur, no matter what the circumstances.

What increases cash flow? And what increases confidence in its stability? These are fundamental questions for building value in businesses.

Increase Net Free Cash Flow

Some ways to increase net free cash flow include sales increases through market share growth, geographic expansion, and new products; margin improvements through better pricing, cost containment, and efficient production; and asset release through efficient use of working capital and reducing (or postponing) capital expenditures.

Increase Stability of Earnings and Cash Flow

Some ways to increase the stability of earnings and cash flow include improved market share; use of noncyclical product lines; a diversified customer base; multiple sources of supply; lower breakeven volume; better external image; stronger internal culture; and more robust organization (not dependent on any one person).

Timing is an Important Factor

Value-building strategies must be matched to the owner's desired time of sale. Depending on the relationship between time and a company's goals and objectives, different value-building strategies will be either more or less effective; ie, what works best within a one- or two-year time frame may not be as effective if it's stretched to four or five years. All strategies do not have the same effectiveness in building value over differing periods of time. To illustrate this, assume that a business owner wants to sell. If the time frame is four to five years, a circumspect program of market share enhancement, even if it requires new investment, might make sense. The objective would be to increase the cash flow by the end of the period, which would help the company attain a higher sales price.

On the other hand, if the time frame is one to two years, the company might be wiser to focus on increasing the stability of cash flows, or creating the perception of increased stability. One way is to hire two vice presidents for sales and give them the responsibility of acting as account representatives handling the company's major clients—which previously the company's owner did. Even though adding two employees might decrease profits, prospective buyers would be impressed that the company's major clients were handled by the organization rather than by an individual. This would influence buyer perception regarding the stability of the company cash flows, and consequently increase the purchase price or improve the terms of the sale.

M&A VALUE BUILDING: UNDERSTAND THE BUYER

Proper value-building strategy is the cornerstone of increasing company worth. "Proper" strategy requires us to differentiate between traditional strategic analysis and value-building analysis. Traditional strategic analysis focuses broadly on improving the long-term prospects of the business. Value-building strategic analysis focuses narrowly on augmenting corporate worth in an M&A marketplace within a given time frame. Although these two kinds of strategic analyses are similar and often yield similar results, the two have a difference that is sometimes subtle and sometimes dramatic.

Building a company's value is a highly customized process. It is influenced by the company's position in its market; trends and issues affecting its industry; and strengths and weaknesses of the competition.

Perhaps most importantly, a company's value-improvement plan should be influenced by the buyers of companies in that industry—and their perceptions of value. Effective and efficient value building means structuring the company to attract the interest of qualified buyers. One should know the needs of likely buyers before beginning value improvement, showing these buyers that the company has what they want. Often, those elements that enhance the worth of the business are not obvious or expected. If owners are not familiar with business buyers, the value-building effort may be difficult at best and misguided and ineffective at worst.

When Geneva conducts value-building services for clients, we go to our buyer database to determine the criteria that buyers desire in a target company. The database contains 10,000 prescreened buyers and tells us the "hot buttons" of each of these buyers.

Buyer hot buttons are different for every industry; however, there are some "common threads" among buyers that seem to transcend company and industry borders. In our work with thousands of middle market buyers, Geneva has identified the following buyer interests:

- Recession resistance—in other words, companies that can survive an economic downturn. This is, of course, an especially high priority for buyers in today's economy. Recession-resistant businesses are popular among buyers because of their stability and low risk. If your industry is naturally sensitive to the economy, look to diversify your markets. Sell to customers who are recession resistant.

- Differentiate your company by offering proprietary products and developing niche markets. This strategy has multiple benefits. First, proprietary products and niche markets usually produce higher profit margins, and buyers will pay higher prices for this added profit-generating potential. Second, there is a greater chance that you will have what the buyer wants if you have a unique product or market. Third, the buyer will have few— if any—other acquisition choices if he wants to acquire the unique product or niche.

    For example, one company we recently sold operated in a mature, low-tech industry. Our client had developed a unique manufacturing process that substantially lowered production costs, which greatly increased the company's value and attractiveness to buyers. The business was sold at a premium to an international manufacturer in the same industry who planned to incorporate the unique manufacturing process into its own operations, producing a company-wide benefit.

As another example, we represented a scientist who had developed a proprietary process capable of saving a specialized industry huge amounts of money annually. Several corporate buyers were interested in purchasing this technology, which was proven in demonstration plans and had already attracted long-term user contracts.

- Incorporate demographic and socio-economic trends into your value building strategy. Buyers are interested in companies that are benefiting from new or emerging trends because they offer above-average growth and profit potential. That's why companies that cater to the elderly population are popular today. Forward-thinking buyers are very much aware of the growth and purchasing power of this sector of the population. Companies involved in environmental products and services are also in high demand. Again, buyers realize the social trend toward environmental awareness, and see opportunity in the growing governmental legislation and regulations that demand environmental protection.

- A "value added" strategy is especially important to wholesalers, distributors, and retailers who look for a product or service that goes beyond the usual scope of service. For instance, wholesalers who are electronically tied to their customers' purchasing system are viewed as having added service and are attractive to buyers.

- Finally, you should run your business as cleanly as possible. Today's buyers carefully scrutinize issues affecting salability, price, and terms. Private business owners run their companies to maximize income and minimize costs. Sometimes that conflicts with the need to run a clean business, yet many buyers, especially large ones, will not consider buying companies with such outstanding issues as unresolved/pending litigation or employee liabilities.

THE M&A MARKETPLACE

The mergers and acquisitions marketplace is burgeoning, a result of nearly every U.S. industry reshaping itself to better compete in today's market. Businesses are challenged by advancing technology, increased foreign and domestic competition, mature markets, and higher customer demands for quality and value. The result is industry cost cutting and consolidation. In response, businesses are looking to mergers and acquisitions as a way to build their competitive strengths and ensure growth.

Reflecting the popularity of M&A as a business growth strategy, the number of announced transactions totaled 2,997 in 1994, the highest figure in seven years. The year ended on an especially strong note, and the trend has continued into 1995. For the first nine months of 1995, 2,528 transactions were announced, a 14 percent increase from the same period in 1994. As is typically the case, most of the M&A activity is occurring in the middle market. Corporate buyers view midsized companies as an opportunity to gain important synergies without "betting the company" on any one acquisition. The middle market offers efficient opportunities for growth while providing a safe harbor from the pitfalls of last decade's megadeals. Seventy-eight percent of the announced transactions in 1993 (where purchase price was disclosed) consisted of deals valued at under $100 million.

The outlook for M&A activity is favorable. Factors driving the increase in business sales—a global marketplace, advancing technology, and consolidating industries—will persist. In addition, buyers are optimistic about the economy, foreign buyers have reappeared, and financing availability and conditions have improved. These and other trends are contributing to a healthy M&A market.

Optimism is a key factor in the surge in M&A activity. CEOs and board members alike are confident about the economy and their business prospects, and regard M&A as an important expansion technique. Subdued during the risky transactions of the 1980s, and cautious during the economic decline of the early 1990s, these buyers have re-entered the market in significant numbers. With these buyers comes a return to basics. Corporate buyers are particularly motivated by strategic acquisitions of close-fitting, synergistic companies. These deals are designed to increase market share, fill voids in the acquiring company's product line, expand geographically, or capitalize on the benefits of shared technologies or vertical integration. Many are pursuing strategic deals as a competitive response to other deals being consummated in their industry. The increase in strategic deals has created a "fear of lost opportunity" among industry participants.

There has also been increased activity from independent owners/operators, financial buyers, and foreign buyers. Supplied by corporate cutbacks among the ranks of middle and upper managers, the pool of quality owners/operators looking to acquire a business has expanded. Independent owners/operators are typically searching for businesses they can own and manage until their retirement. These individuals are looking for acquisitions in which they can leverage their experience to grow the company.

Financial buyers are also back, enjoying added funding by investors looking for higher yield investments such as business acquisitions. Investors, in search of higher returns than those afforded by interest-bearing instruments, are looking to invest in growing companies. Finally, foreign buyers are also returning to the marketplace. In fact, the first nine months of 1994 showed a 10 percent increase over the same period in 1993 in the number of foreign buyers. As Europe's recession recedes and the value of the dollar declines, U.S. assets will become even more affordable to foreign buyers (see Fig. 10.1).

Finally, today's increased M&A activity is being supported by a lending environment that is conducive to transactions. Banks are looking for new sources of revenue and are attracted to the high-margin business of M&A financing. As a result, financing terms have eased, and lenders are willing to relax financial requirements and consider synergies in order to complete deals.

In summary, the M&A market is favorable. It is being bolstered by earnest interest from strategic buyers, the need for companies to make acquisitions as a growth strategy in our slow-growth economy, and the loosening of financial markets.

STRATEGY FORMULATION

Having reviewed the basics of value and value building, now consider how corporate strategy is formulated. The classic process calls for mapping a firm's comparative strengths and weaknesses with market opportunities and problems in order to develop strategies for achieving long-term goals and short-term objectives. From this comes a list of possibilities for building a company's value. Competing policies are subjected to rigorous evaluation, using a test to help make the strategic choice.

Three keys to strategic management are:

- Creativity promotes strategy formulation.
- Consistency directs strategy evaluation.
- Structure controls implementation of strategy.

Strategy, however, has a dark side. It can fool executives into thinking they have a good grip on a situation when they do not have much of a

FIGURE 10.1

Who Is Buying? (1/92–5/94)

Under $3 million

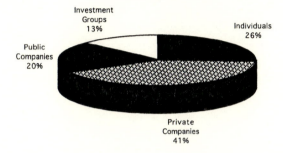

Investment Groups 13%

Individuals 26%

Public Companies 20%

Private Companies 41%

$3 - $10 million

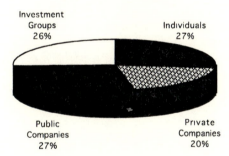

Investment Groups 26%

Individuals 27%

Public Companies 27%

Private Companies 20%

Over $10 million

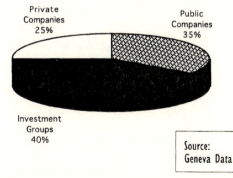

Private Companies 25%

Public Companies 35%

Investment Groups 40%

Source: Geneva Data

handle on anything. At times, the more sophisticated the strategy, the stronger the strategic illusion. Many companies have suffered terrible reverses, even though they had what seemed to be adequate strategic planning.

To be truly effective, strategic thinking must anticipate the unanticipated and foresee the unforeseen. Strategy plays no part if everything is assumed to be known and a company's future is expected to emulate its past. Companies committed to building value must plan for the unplanned and accept radical change where needed.

Value-building strategies position a company within its industry in order to generate optimum cash flows and to protect those flows from disruption. The key to success is to search for early signs of opportunity the company can exploit and early warnings of problems so the company can adapt.

Awareness of company strengths and weaknesses can dramatically increase future cash flows and make them less vulnerable to fluctuation. Ideally, a company should build on its strengths and eliminate its weaknesses. But in the real world, this is often impossible. In fact, if a company tries to make everything better, it will wind up making nothing better. It is frequently better to select a few strengths and weaknesses on which to concentrate, focusing on taking advantage of strengths rather than shoring up weaknesses (unless, of course, they threaten the company). Strengths are what generate revenue and profits. Weaknesses are often more theoretical or psychological than operational or financial.

HOW STRATEGY BUILDS VALUE

In planning value-building strategies, it is important to balance risk with reward so that the essential business is never threatened. The hallmark of good strategy is optimizing reward with minimum risks. A thorough strategic planning program that combines possible strategies for building value with an assessment of implementation problems should be part of every value-building program.

Good strategy is the most efficient way to build company value. By doing the "right things," executives will gain substantial leverage. Rather than scattering their efforts on activities that will have minimal impact on ultimate value, they learn to focus their energies on activities that will have the greatest impact on value—in essence, giving them the "biggest bang for their buck."

It has been said that it's better to do the right things wrong than the wrong things right. So often in business, a great deal of sincere effort is wasted on activities that have little impact on building actual value in companies. These activities may not be wrong as in "bad"; rather, they are "wrong" in that they do not enhance corporate wealth. Most business executives spend the majority of their time on day-to-day operational issues that have little impact on what their businesses are worth today or what they could be worth in the future. The "right things" are those activities that focus on increasing value and wealth—those strategic factors, financial characteristics, and corporate qualities that serious buyers weigh heavily in assessing what price they will pay for companies.

THE VALUE-BUILDING PROCESS

Every company has its own unique combination of value-improvement strategies. A standard process can help identify those strategies. Here is how we develop value-building strategies for our clients at Geneva:

- We begin the process by determining exit goals. These help identify appropriate strategies. We ask such questions such as, "How much do you want for the company?" and "How long will it be before you sell?"

- To build value, it's important to know where a company is deficient. We perform a detailed diagnostic of the company that reveals its strengths and weaknesses—value-enhancers and risk considerations—from a buyer's perspective. Many times we uncover considerations about which the company wasn't aware.

- Once we identify concerns, we can develop an M&A action plan. This "packaging" of a company for sale is critical. It can be the difference between getting a premium price or a discounted price, a ready sale or a long period of time languishing in the market.

- We prepare a complete strategic and financial analysis to help determine the current value of the company and develop effective value-building strategies. Part of this exercise involves manipulating certain financial and operating characteristics of the business and measuring their effect on future value.

- Because the value-building process may have an impact on the exit plan, depending on the current value and the complexity of the value improvement program, we may then recommend a change in the owner's exit goals.

VALUE-BUILDING IDEAS FOR YOUR COMPANY

If you are planning to sell your business within the next two to five years, you should begin building value today so you can get the highest possible price at sale time. This may mean changing the way you run your business, because running a business well and preparing for a successful sale are *not* the same thing, although they have much in common.

Remember, the best way to prepare for sale is to enhance your bottom line. Buyers pay premiums for profitable companies. The higher the *amount* and *certainty* of future free cash flow, and the better the historical profit *trend*, the more buyers will pay, and the less structure or deferred payments they will attach to the deal.

As you nurture profits, don't ignore the operational details of the business—because buyers won't! The merger mania of the 1980s left many overzealous buyers with companies full of problems, and today's buyers are more cautious, taking time to perform detailed discovery and analyses before making an offer. And they either steer clear or offer less for companies with unresolved issues.

Although the steps necessary to prepare your business for sale will be specific to your company, remember that building a business to maximize value is not always the same as just building a better business. Here are five steps for preparing your business for sale, along with some of their embedded subtleties:

Avoid Long Payback Investments

Building the value of your business may mean canceling some of your business plans. If you want to sell the company within the next few years, you should avoid investing in projects with long payback periods. Examples include investments in new facilities or R&D funds to develop new products. Such investments in the future usually negatively impact short-term profits, both in terms of cash expenditures and diversion of management time. These are the same profit figures buyers will use to determine the price they are willing to pay for the company. To obtain the optimum value, you should maximize profits just prior to sale.

Plan for Organizational Succession

While entrepreneurs understand the need for a strong organization, too many fail to construct an organization that can operate without them. Buyers are very wary of such businesses, especially if the company depends on the owner/entrepreneur to generate sales. A buyer needs assurance that the business can continue to operate smoothly upon sale, and that customers will not leave when the current management sells. You must clear the way for a seamless ownership transition by replacing your efforts with those of managers and salespeople who will remain with the business after the sale.

Alter Your Financial Management

When Geneva markets a company, we recast the financial statements to show the true profit-earning potential of the business. The hard part is persuading the buyer that the recast items are "real." One way to avoid the issue and also ensure a higher value is to actually operate the company in a recasted manner prior to selling. This may entail removing family members from the payroll, reducing owners' perks, writing off bad inventory so inventory turns improve, clearing payables of delinquencies, collecting or writing off late receivables, and eliminating nonoperating assets and liabilities from the balance sheet. However, be aware that improving profits is a balancing act. While buyers will be attracted to higher profits, they will want assurances of the company's future well-being. They will be suspicious of cuts in vital areas such as R&D, plant and equipment maintenance, and advertising. Such cost-cutting measures could have long-term negative effects on the business, for which buyers may discount the price they are willing to pay.

Resolve Business Issues

Resolving your business issues may seem like an obvious way to prepare for a sale, but what about the business issues of neighboring companies? Most owners realize that unresolved or pending litigation, unfulfilled tax obligations, OSHA violations, and inadequate insurance coverage are common deal issues, but may overlook another very important one: EPA violations. EPA regulations are becoming more and more pervasive at both the state and federal levels. If your business is subject to such regulations, buyers may want proof that the company meets all EPA standards. They may also require proof that *neighboring companies* are not polluting your property through such problems as leaky underground pipes or underground storage tanks. Even the banks involved in today's deal transactions are requiring full knowledge of all EPA violations. If any are discovered, whether they originated at your plant or at your neighbor's, they may delay or even terminate the deal. Better to resolve such business issues prior to entering the marketplace, rather than risk losing interested buyers.

Adjust Your Product Mix

The obvious strategy is to emphasize sales of higher margin products already in your product line. You may also be able to provide an immediate boost as well as a long-term advantage to profits by exploiting those products that differentiate you from competitors. Buyers will pay for such uniqueness, as well as the stability it may bring to future cash flows.

Once again, a key to preparing your company for sale is to evaluate the business through the eyes of a buyer. Focus on improving the amount and stability of future cash flows, but don't ignore the details behind the profits. Buyers will be just as interested in the business decisions that shape the company as they are in its bottom line.

VALUE-BUILDING EXAMPLES

Just as value is very subjective, depending on the buyer, value building is very customized, depending on the company. This is illustrated in Table 10.4.

All came to Geneva intending to sell, but none were satisfied with their original values. Instead, they chose to implement value-building techniques designed just for them. The audio tape case manufacturer was in the midst of a dramatic growth phase and felt he could achieve a higher value. The problem was that he was personally responsible for most of the company's sales. Based on this, a buyer would not be comfortable in the stability of sales and cash flow after the owner left the business. The client implemented an aggressive, diversified sales effort that diffused his importance. Then he hired a high-powered sales manager to take over sales.

TABLE 10.4

Value-Building Examples ($ millions)

Company	Original Value	Value-Building Techniques	Post Value-Building Value
Manufacture audio tape cases	11.0	Aggressive sales effort Sales manager Incentive compensation	18.0
Manufacture ball bearings	3.2	Niche vs. commodity JIT Service vs. price Pre-tax from 12% to 20%	6.5
Manufacture valves & fittings	5.0	Market opportunity New marketing campaign	10.0

Source:
Geneva Data

Not only did this strategy reassure potential buyers, it also freed the owner to concentrate on other areas of the business. Realizing that sales growth was only half the formula, the owner implemented a successful incentive compensation plan that contained costs and helped to fund the growth, thereby preserving the company's balance sheet. In just two years, the company's value dramatically improved, and Geneva sold the business for 64 percent more than its original value.

The ball bearings manufacturer had a different problem. He manufactured a commodity product and had stagnant sales and declining margins. His strategy was to begin offering rapid service to manufacturers. By adjusting operations to accommodate short runs, the company was able to satisfy the quick-turn requirements of the market. Rather than competing on price, the company competed on service, and was able to raise prices for the value it now added. Pretax profits increased from 12 percent of sales to nearly 20 percent. In turn, value rose 103 percent.

The third company is a good example of how to take advantage of changing market trends. This company's core product line was fabricated steel valves for water systems. When clean water legislation called for the use of fabricated steel values to replace the weaker cast-iron valves in common use, the company capitalized on its position in the valve market and implemented an aggressive marketing program. The result was higher sales, improved profits, and a 100 percent increase in value.

SUMMARY

While value building is a complex process, any company can do it. The greatest drawback is time. Give yourself enough time to have a substantive effect on value by beginning the process well in advance of marketing the company for sale.

11

Adding Value to Companies Through Strategic Alliances and Partnerships

Jana B. Matthews

Strategic alliances and partnerships can offer substantial benefits to both entrepreneurial companies and large corporations. These alliances enable partners to offset their respective strengths and weaknesses, hence creating an arrangement that is mutually beneficial. A value chain assessment can help the small and large company select the best partners.

To get a partnership off to a good start, start with a small project to evaluate how well the partners work together and whether the partnership should be maintained. A multi-phased project provides the opportunities to work out small problems before they become major problems.

The guiding principles of partnership arrangements include practicing a partnership mentality in which both partners act as equals; creating two teams of champions to provide continuity over the long run; communicating frequently with the partner in order to avoid surprises; engaging in joint problem solving; and, finally, thinking and planning long term but delivering something tangible in the short term.

Partnerships have advantages and disadvantages. The key

to partnership success is to have complementary dissimilarities. The goal should be to learn how to capitalize on, learn
from, and enjoy these differences.

In a 1993 Coopers & Lybrand survey of 400 CEOs of product and services
companies with annual revenues of $1 million to $50 million, more than
half (55 percent) said they are currently involved in an average of three
strategic alliances. They reported that since entering strategic alliances,
their revenues are up 11 percent, and they are growing at a rate 20 percent
faster than companies not engaged in alliances. In recent years, many
entrepreneurs have begun to recognize that partnerships and strategic alliances with large companies are viable strategies to build their own companies and complete their value chains.

Encouragingly, large and small companies are finding it mutually beneficial to work together. When they partner, they can help compensate for
each other's weaknesses, and provide growth opportunities and entry into
new markets. They can share marketing and promotion arrangements, and
selling and distribution channels; improve products; and incur less financial risk than they would if they tried to do this by themselves.

USING A VALUE CHAIN ASSESSMENT TO HELP
FIND THE RIGHT PARTNER

Entrepreneurs interested in forming a strategic alliance should first
complete a value chain assessment to help identify their own strengths
and weaknesses, and potential partners and problems that may occur.

For example, a smaller company's strengths may be research or manufacturing in small quantity. A big company may not be able to accommodate small orders in its large-scale manufacturing environment. The
smaller company's problem may be marketing and finding appropriate
distribution channels to reach customers. The big company's problem may
be having enough products to market and sell through their existing distribution channels. By partnering, the large company acquires more products and the small company gains access to a large distribution system.

It's important to identify and partner with a company that can compensate for your company's weaknesses. The objective is to maximize the
value of the business by reducing the amount of financial outlay, getting

products developed, and to market, and getting the highest possible return on equity or dollars invested.

FINDING THE RIGHT PARTNER

The challenge for small companies with good ideas and the ability to maneuver quickly is to persuade big companies that a partnership will be mutually beneficial. Finding the right partner requires time and sustained, systematic effort.

Don't look for just any partner. Identify companies that have strengths that will offset your firm's weaknesses and where your company can provide value the other firm needs. Think about the size of the potential partner, their location, and whether or not they are amenable to the concept of partnering. Develop a profile of the "ideal" partner.

Once you have identified and screened a company, make sure you get good legal counsel and protect your intellectual property, but do not turn the negotiations over to the lawyers. The negotiating activities and discussions provide an important platform in which strong partnerships can be built.

` Lawyers have a lot to offer in terms of helping to explain the risks, protecting intellectual property, and offering advice on strategy. Since entrepreneurs tend to be optimists, refusing to believe anything can stop them and underestimating what can go wrong, lawyers can help them avoid potential pitfalls. However, there are few advantages and many disadvantages to letting lawyers negotiate the terms and conditions of the partnership or alliance.

GETTING THE PARTNERSHIP OFF TO A GOOD START

At the beginning of a partnership, start simple. Vision and confidence are important, but a series of finite projects successfully completed will provide momentum and opportunities to evaluate the partnership and determine whether to move ahead, change direction, or cut losses and terminate the partnership. It's extremely important to define individual roles and responsibilities, so if problems occur it will be relatively easy to determine what went wrong, what needs to be fixed, and who will fix it.

FOUR GUIDING PRINCIPLES OF THE PARTNERSHIP ARRANGEMENT

Once a partnership has been launched, four principles should guide the relationship:

Practice a Partnership Mentality

This is quite different from a customer/supplier mentality. Even though a small company isn't really equal to the large company in terms of size and scope, it brings value to the partnership. Presumably the complementary strengths and weaknesses are what attracted the companies to form a partnership in the first place. Recognizing their mutual dependency, and the need for both to be successful, is key to negotiating and managing a successful partnership.

Develop a Team of Champions

Remember that rising stars in the company may rise right out of the firmament. They go to other companies, get promoted somewhere else in the corporation, or take early retirement. If more than one person at each company is involved in the partnership arrangement, the alliance is much stronger than if a single person is championing it or responsible for its success.

Communicate Frequently with the Partnership Company

Communications must flow freely, including the good and bad news. There can be no surprises in a partnership. Joint problem solving is the hallmark of a strong alliance. The array of solutions is much richer than either company could develop alone, and the resulting synergy of the two companies is what makes partnerships and alliances so popular.

Plan Long Term; Deliver Short Term

Although hopes are that the alliance will be long term, short-term successes are essential. Given the pace of change, corporations are no longer willing to "hang in," waiting for a home run. A series of base hits is required now. The key to a successful partnership is a series of smaller successes that, together, advance each company and the partnership to their long-term goals.

PITFALLS OF PARTNERSHIPS

Partnerships have a tremendous upside, but they also have a downside, which if not managed, can create major problems.

Trust is an extremely important issue. Small companies sometimes worry that large companies will steal or pirate away their technology, product, or people. The large company, on the other hand, worries that the small company, because of its youth, size, or financial condition, won't be able to deliver on an agreement. For example, if the small company has only one manufacturing facility, corporate executives are concerned about entering a relationship that requires the small company to deliver products from a single plant. What if something happens to the plant? What if the small company isn't financially strong enough to be around next year to manufacture the product?

A large company can get ripped off because it has deep pockets. AT&T teamed with a small company that was supposedly in the pay phone business. The small company didn't pan out. Because AT&T was a partner, some of the people who invested in the small company sued AT&T, which they assumed had performed the necessary due diligence, and AT&T ended up paying $10 million to settle their lawsuits.

Control is another major issue. The large company may think it should control everything. After all, it's successful and has more resources than the small company. But entrepreneurs typically score very high on the dominance scale and often start companies because they want more control. A struggle over which company controls which aspects of the alliance often is an issue that needs to be addressed during the negotiations.

Failure is also an issue. Very few executives in large companies are rewarded for failures. Entrepreneurs can tolerate much more failure, hence they are willing to take risks. Examining tolerance for risk and failure is also essential during the negotiations.

Large and small companies often have differing perceptions of time. When an entrepreneur says "I'll get right back to you," that usually means hours or days because decisions can be made quickly. However, when a corporate executive uses these words, it can mean weeks or months. Delays can be caused by people going on vacation, the requirement to check the idea with several managers, needing to get a decision from somewhere else in the organization, checking the idea with corporate counsel, interruption due to corporate reorganization, or a myriad of other distractions.

Both companies must come to an agreement concerning the value of what each brings to the partnership, as well as the financial value. A new idea or product prototype is necessary but not sufficient to get a new product to market. It will take 10 to 20 times the initial investment to get the product to the market. Hence, it's not just what the idea is worth, but also how much more money must be expended to complete the value chain that determines the value or worth of the product. Typically, the farther along the value chain and the less that has to be spent to get the customer to buy products and get a return on investment, the more valuable the concept and the higher the valuation.

Compensation can be another major issue. When a partnership is being negotiated, some corporate executives are reluctant to negotiate an agreement where entrepreneurs make more than they do. But it's essential to maintain the focus on the companies, the alliance, and the financial upside that will be created for both companies. The redistribution of that money is a separate issue. Large companies, with many employees and stockholders, have a larger base for redistribution. Entrepreneurial companies, with fewer employees and stockholders have a smaller base, hence each person should receive more compensation commensurate with the greater risk that each has taken.

HOW ALLIANCES ADD VALUE TO THE ENTREPRENEURIAL COMPANY

Partnerships and strategic alliances can be very beneficial for entrepreneurs. They may gain new knowledge and expertise, new products and processes, and new ways of manufacturing and fabricating. The entrepreneurial company may also benefit from faster manufacturing and distribution.

Cash flow problems are reduced because the alliance provides an infusion of money, and the value chain can be completed more quickly.

Along with learning collaboration skills, the entrepreneurial company gains a window into the partner's corporate culture, which allows networking and may even result in a merger or acquisition sometime in the future.

Finally, much faster growth can be expected. Companies that enter into strategic alliances tend to have significantly faster growth rates than those that don't.

LEARNING TO ENJOY THE DIFFERENCES

A word of caution: For the partnership to work, both parties must recognize the importance of complementary dissimilarities. Unless each partner has something the other wants, there's no basis for the partnership. The trick is to recognize and learn how to capitalize on, learn from, and enjoy these differences.

BIBLIOGRAPHY

Barley, Stephen R., John Freeman, and Ralph C. Hybels. "Strategic Alliances in Commercial Biotechnology." In *Networks and Organizations,* edited by R. Eccles and N. Norhia. Boston: Harvard Business School Press, forthcoming.

Botkin, James W., and Jana Matthews. *Winning Combinations.* New York: John Wiley, 1992.

Burrill, G. Steven, and Kenneth B. Lee, Jr. *Biotech 91: A Changing Environment.* San Francisco: Ernst & Young, 1990.

Hooper, Lawrence. "Big Blue Cultivates New Markets by Thinking Small," *The Wall Street Journal,* February 27, 1991, B2.

"How Strategic Alliances Grow Companies," *Coopers & Lybrand, Growing Your Business* (September/October 1993): 8–10.

Sharp, Margaret. "David, Goliath, and the Biotechnology Business," *The OECD Observer* (June–July 1990): 22–24.

"Sony Adopts Strategy to Broaden Ties with Small Firms," *The Wall Street Journal,* February 28, 1991, B2.

Tuite, Robert. "Strategies for Technology-Based New Business Development." Paper delivered at the International Forum on Technology Management, Brussels, Belgium, June 1989.

12

Report from the Entrepreneurial Front Line: Developing Value Through Strategic Alliances

Edward Payne

Ed Payne, Bernie Perry, and Terry Walker started a new company, Gateway Technologies, to introduce products using microPCM, a fabric with greatly enhanced thermal properties, to the marketplace. These principals of Gateway knew nothing about the chemical and textile industries, but were excited about the product and determined to be successful.

They quickly learned that technology transfer is more than just a sales and marketing effort. To be successful in this process, the firm must control the development and testing of the initial product *and* introduce it to the marketplace.

After a series of attempts and false assumptions, and after a thorough education in how the textile industry works, they made some progress. By utilizing the value chain and by developing value through strategic alliances, the principals made the right connections. In the process, it became necessary to restructure the company and utilize a new technological procedure to overcome problems with the reaction time of fiber/chemical companies. Gateway has now arranged for testing protocol, developed agreements with several product manufacturers, and expects to soon have products for sale to the public.

This is the story of three entrepreneurs who stumbled on a breakthrough technology, acquired it, marketed it to an industry they knew nothing about, encountered predictable problems, refocused, persevered, and finally succeeded.

How? By developing significant value through strategic alliances.

MICROPCM TECHNOLOGY

It all started in early 1990 when I saw a demonstration of a new technology that the inventor had been unable to license.

The new discovery was a fabric with greatly enhanced thermal properties. To produce it, microencapsulated phase change material (microPCM) is mixed in the chemical solution of a man-made fiber. When the fiber is extruded, the thermal-enhancing materials are contained inside the fiber itself. The fibers provide greater insulation protection than any leading brand of textile insulation.

The product looked promising and the inventor was ready to license. The question for me was: How does one introduce a new technology into a marketplace he or she knows nothing about?

Opportunities come in strange packages and in many forms. Within a few months, I was in the process of building a new business.

THE FOUNDING OF GATEWAY TECHNOLOGIES

Several advisors responded positively to the technology and its patented application and encouraged me to take it to the marketplace even though I lacked experience in the chemical and textile industries. I brought in my first partner, who had recently returned to the United States after successfully managing a firm in Saudi Arabia for nine years. He had experienced the success of building a new company and was interested in being part of a new company built around the microPCM technology.

At the same time, an attorney friend with a chemical background looked at the technology and responded positively. He was very impressed with the microPCM technology and felt it could be successfully transferred to the chemical and textile industries. He became the third partner.

In August 1990, we obtained a license from TRDC, and Gateway Technologies was formed. Our combined management team had experience in marketing and sales, business foundation and growth, and legal counsel. We still lacked experience in the chemical and textile industry, so we involved an advisor with that experience.

LEARNING THE REALITIES OF TECHNOLOGY TRANSFER

Achieving the technology transfer by forming strategic alliances with companies in the chemical and textile industries seemed to be our best strategy for success. We believed that our marketing and sales experience provided the background needed to successfully transfer technology. However, technology transfer is more than just a sales and marketing effort. To effect a transfer, it is necessary to assume control of the process of developing and testing the first product and introducing it to the marketplace, rather than relying on the strategic alliances to do this. The advisor who had experience with large textile companies provided invaluable insight. We created an advisory board the members of which had expertise in the textile industry, patents, and corporate finance.

ESTABLISHING MANAGEMENT RESPONSIBILITIES

With the team established, our next task was to determine responsibilities. As president and CEO, I was responsible for company strategy and completing the business plan. Preparation of the plan required seven months due to the lack of familiarity with the industry. The textile industry is not neatly organized; rather, it is highly fragmented. People in the industry for years still hadn't figured it out. Most only understood the level directly above them and the level directly below them.

For example, fabrics are made from fibers, or yarns containing fibers; yet a vice president of a major fiber-producing chemical company advised us that his company didn't consider itself part of the textile industry. That made as much sense as not considering a starting pitcher a member of a baseball team. If the pitcher doesn't throw the ball, and if a chemical company doesn't make fiber, nothing happens.

Anyway, one thing we learned was how the textile industry value chain works, and that knowledge has been a valuable company asset.

SALES

Since the goal was to be the first product to the marketplace, the challenge for the sales area was to find the company that would do this. To identify that company, the following steps were taken:

- company research
- targeted direct mail
- follow-up phone calls to discuss benefits of the technology with the company
- sharing of additional nonconfidential information, if necessary
- obtaining letter of interest from the company
- executing a confidentiality agreement
- arranging a visit
- giving additional confidential information
- hands-on demonstration of technology
- negotiating an evaluation agreement
- executing a license agreement for the specific product
- introducing the product to the marketplace.

LEGAL COUNSEL

Legal counsel was responsible for structuring legal agreements and assisting with both strategy and tactics. After a group discussion, counsel would incorporate our decisions into legal agreements. We established a relationship with a large law firm that reviewed all draft legal agreements. The agreements included:

- confidentiality
- evaluation

- development
- close-down of negotiations
- license
- consulting

VALUE CHAIN ASSESSMENT OF GATEWAY'S STRENGTHS AND WEAKNESSES

"Value chain" is the process by which a new idea gets to market, or it's a series of linked stages over which value is added to a product as it makes its way from invention to final distribution. The value chain is comprised of the following:

- research
- development
- design
- manufacturing
- marketing
- sales
- distribution

When the firm started, each team member had some experience with each step of the value chain, mostly in marketing and sales. None had any experience in the textile industry. But determination and enthusiasm prevailed. This technology and its application offered the chance of a lifetime. Marketing the technology was going to be exciting, and if successful, the prize for the effort could be awesome.

What were numerous and obvious weaknesses to outsiders were, to the team, minor inconveniences that could be overcome. The approach was to get started and make adjustments along the way.

One primary goal was to get the first product to the marketplace. Our inexperience in the chemical and textile industries resulted in a significant amount of detailed discussions. To maintain focus, we carried out role play activities with one member always playing the part of the chemical or textile company so we would better understand that company's position. We reached consensus on the strategy after thorough discussion and by using as much common sense as possible.

THE SEARCH FOR STRATEGIC PARTNERS

Gateway's textile value chain consisted of:

- phase change material manufacturers
- microcapsule manufacturers
- fiber/chemical companies
- yarn manufacturers
- textile mill fabric manufacturers
- end-use product manufacturers
- the distribution system

Our plan was to search for strategic partners to make up the various levels of the textile value chain. They would need to complete specific-applications R&D so a license agreement could be developed to introduce new products to the marketplace.

The search for strategic partners started in the business school at our local university by identifying 200 companies that seemed like possible partners.

INITIATING A DIRECT MAIL CAMPAIGN

We mailed a circular introducing the technology and the company to each target company. Our intention was to call each company approximately 10 days after we mailed our information. Instead, on the seventh day, the phone started ringing off the hook. Business had begun. Within a short period of time, we received a 17 percent response to the direct mail campaign, and the percentage kept increasing.

One objective of the direct mail campaign was to obtain letters of interest from companies confirming their belief in a desired product. To date, we have more than 100 letters of interest from chemical/textile companies around the world. Of course, letters of interest don't directly result in an equal number of licenses, but they are a beginning.

The next step was to get additional information about an interested company in order to better understand their potential role in the strategic alliance. A confidentiality agreement was needed to proceed to the next important step of face-to-face discussions.

Reaching the key people in an organization was fairly easy, but once the confidentiality agreements were discussed, there was a built-in speed brake. Time does not have the same meaning to small and large companies. With few exceptions, the larger the company, the longer it took to get anything accomplished.

To date, we have executed more than 80 confidentiality agreements with companies throughout the textile value chain, and they have taken anywhere from one to 12 months to complete. We used a boilerplate confidentiality agreement, modified as necessary to accommodate the specific concerns of each company. On a few occasions, companies have insisted on the use of their formatted agreements. This was not objectionable as long as key provisions were included.

INITIAL EXCITEMENT—THEN LETDOWN

One of the first chemical companies we contacted called within three days of receiving the letter. Several days later, after a visit by two top officials, they assigned a project manager to the technology.

Then nothing happened for the next 18 months. We learned that no matter how interested a textile mill or an end-use product manufacturer was about the prospects of the technology and how it could add value to their products, if they didn't manufacture one of the six major man-made fibers, their ability to move ahead was dependent on a fiber/chemical company making the microPCM fiber.

We shifted our focus from textile mills and end-use product manufacturers to the few dozen fiber companies in the United States, Europe, and Japan who were near the beginning of the textile value chain. After visiting Gateway, most were very impressed with the technology and some expressed great interest in adding a high-valued product to their existing commodity business.

TRYING TO GET COMPANIES TO COMMIT

Still in spite of the interest, the technology transfer marketing efforts started to grind to a halt because not one of the fiber/chemical companies committed to buying a small sample of microPCMs to put in their chem-

ical solutions and extrude the fiber. It began to look as though each fiber/
chemical company was afraid to make this decision, even though great
interest existed throughout the textile industry.

FINALLY—A BREAKTHROUGH

One major U.S. fiber/chemical company said, "Bring us the market and
bring us the money, and we'll do it." We did a strategy refocus in order
to do just that by asking a major end-use product manufacturer to buy a
small sample of microPCMs and then use their influence to get the same
fiber supplier to make prototype fiber. The prototype fiber was successfully
created and a prototype product was successfully fabricated. Initial tests
were positive and very encouraging to both partners.

When a second batch of microPCM fiber was requested from the fiber/
chemical company, the end-use product company was advised that the
decision would be made by the fiber company's corporate offices. Months
later, the fiber chemical company still liked the technology, wanted to
finish developing the technology in their fiber, and wanted a license—but,
they indicated, at a later time.

After three years of discussions with this particular fiber/chemical company, two senior representatives of the fiber/chemical company visited
Gateway. Their reaction was, "We can't believe we didn't do business with
you three years ago." They returned to their boss recommending that their
company move full speed ahead.

WHAT'S HOLDING US BACK

As for all the other companies, it was obvious that there were problems
in communicating with large companies or that all the visionaries and risk-
takers were busy attending to other affairs.

In defense of these big companies, many firms just don't know how to
deal with an entrepreneurial three-person company. One advisor said that
a big chemical company couldn't treat Gateway like a normal company
because it didn't perform like any "normal" company. An example given
was that we were undercapitalized and couldn't send sample microPCMs.

In addition, fiber/chemical companies had a legitimate concern that
the technology would force them to change their testing discipline,

which could result in producing an inferior product with their name on it.

Discussions have been held with more than 150 American and 40 European and Japanese companies. All are interested in the potential added value the technology can bring to their products. We have dozens of testimonials about the technology and its value. If nothing else, these third-party comments provide the motivation to hang in there.

DECIDING ON OUR FIRST MAJOR STRATEGY CHANGE

Some of our frustration with the lack of movement on the part of the fiber/chemical companies was relieved during the summer of 1992. Our licensor had filed a patent to topically coat fabrics with microPCMs. This would relieve the problem of dealing with the slow-moving fiber/chemical companies. We contacted a number of textile mills and other non-fiber producing companies about evaluating our technology topically by utilizing their coating processes to serve as the carrier medium for the microPCMs. We expected to satisfy the missing link: the completion of specific-applications R&D.

To date, 15 topical evaluation agreements have been executed to develop the following products utilizing the technology: blankets, gloves, boot/shoe liners, medical drapes, laminated fabrics, stretch fabrics, and composite materials.

Once the first development project began, a major glitch was discovered. The textile company could coat a fabric, but lacked the thermodynamic expertise to understand, modify, or decide on the next step. The difference with the thermally enhanced fabric could be felt, but standard thermal tests and procedures to define what was actually happening with the inclusion of the technology could not be applied.

The assumption that the textile companies had heat-flow expertise readily available within was erroneous. This stumbling block put the evaluation agreements on hold until this new problem could be solved.

RESTRUCTURING THE VALUE CHAIN STRATEGIC ALLIANCE STRATEGY

Meanwhile, we sought the advice of several experts whose opinions we trusted on the following question: "If Gateway is to be restructured, what advice would you give on the process?" Here is a brief analysis of the most mentioned recommendations:

- Gateway must take control.
- Pick a niche and provide a product.
- A marketplace exists that sees the product's value, but the fiber is not getting to them.
- Time has been spent building relationships with people who aren't sure what they're going to get or when they're going to get it.
- Develop contract manufacturing relationships and don't go into manufacturing yourselves.
- Product tests will evolve over time. A product doesn't have to be perfect to launch.

After considering each of these comments, we scheduled a small meeting with our advisory board. We reached a consensus that Gateway needed to restructure. Progress had been moving forward and the feeling was that success would eventually come, but the longer it took to succeed, the easier it would be for investors to believe it was not going to happen and the easier it was for a textile mill or end-use product manufacturer to lose faith in Gateway's ability to deliver the fiber or fabric. By restructuring, the process could be accelerated and we could still form strategic alliances to assist in achieving the goals. The new focus was summarized in this way:

- Gateway will become more proactive, assume control, and take the leadership role of developing and introducing the first product to the marketplace. We will sell thermally enhanced fibers and fabrics.
- Gateway will establish control over the thermal testing protocols required during the development and certification of products utilizing our technology.

SATISFYING OUR OBJECTIVES

To satisfy the second objective of the new focus, we needed to recruit someone who had both product development and technical expertise to serve as the technical member of the management team. This person would become the technical link in guiding product development between Gateway and a testing facility, and identified product manufacturers. We brought on a former senior executive with a chemical firm who had diversified experience in managing research and development and new business development. This new consulting team member had special skills in managing technology and innovation, strategic planning, technology transfer, joint venture formation, and creating new business opportunities.

We reached an agreement with one of the best facilities in the United States and another one in Germany to develop the testing protocol needed to produce a specification sheet about the product.

One of the topical-coating textile mills we originally approached has finished their prototype fabric development. The results were exciting to all parties, and sample fabric has been supplied to Gateway and made available to more than a dozen product manufacturers with development agreements to fabricate various prototype products. The product manufacturers pay for product testing at selected partner facilities and conduct in-house testing. Once each product manufacturer is satisfied, licenses are executed to introduce specific products to their respective niches in the marketplace.

WATCHING OUR STRATEGY START TO WORK

Our original attempts to locate a chemical company willing to spend its own money had been futile, then things started to change. We recontacted a number of fiber/chemical companies—not as sellers of technology, but as customers. This new approach was conducted to determine what it would cost to contract with each specific chemical company to develop the microPCM fiber and sell it to Gateway to supply to the licensees. A major chemical company agreed to develop the technology inside a major man-made fiber. By the time their development program is finished, our company restructuring will have paved the product-introduction trail.

This new approach, whereby partners would solve the technology challenge and Gateway would solve the market development challenge, seems to have made a big difference on each chemical company's thought process. As a result of this new approach, small samples of microPCMs have been supplied to three additional acrylic fiber chemical companies—one Japanese manufacturer, one European manufacturer, and one American manufacturer. Just as soon as each company checks on the compatibility of the microPCMs with the chemicals each uses to make their acrylic fibers, quotes on the development and production costs will be provided. One of the American fiber manufacturers does not need sample microPCMs because they already have experience making this fiber.

When the first successful samples of microPCM acrylic fiber have been received as a result of the better-late-than-never strategy, the strategic partners will produce and test numerous thermally enhanced products.

This will trigger the development of a multitude of additional products. In order to maintain control of the trademark and to meet the advertising challenge presented by so many different products, we have contracted with an advertising company experienced in the textile industry. A coordinated communication and advertising campaign is planned for the not-too-distant future.

NEW SOURCES OF FINANCING

The original business plan called for a few hundred thousand dollars in order to generate tens of millions of dollars. Only a small part of that was actually raised. That may be because potential investors recognized that a few problems had not been addressed. These problems have now been eliminated. The new business plan focuses on the need for a few million dollars—which may be able to generate hundreds of millions of dollars. It also focuses on completing the management team. The new business plan will be used to approach the sophisticated venture capital community that recognizes it takes money to make money.

THE LIGHT AT THE END OF THE TUNNEL

All partners have received quite an education over the last four years from the chemical and textile industries, the advisors, and the school of hard knocks. The company now has significant value because of the strategic alliances and because of our ability to:

- persevere
- identify a need in the marketplace
- document more than 150 companies interested in applying the technology
- identify, understand, and link each level of the textile value chain

- assume the leadership role and serve as a catalyst between each level of the textile value chain (by selling thermally enhanced fibers and fabrics)
- manage development of the technology by creating sound legal agreements with strategic partners
- see the big picture and simultaneously manage each part of the puzzle

It seems that all of the critical strategic alliances are finally in place. Not only can we see the light at the end of the tunnel, but maybe Gateway has just climbed on board the train en route to the promised land. Hallelujah!

Index

About the Contributors, Sponsors, and Editors

CONTRIBUTORS

LEE G. BOLMAN, Ph.D., holds the Marion Bloch Chair in Leadership at the Henry W. Bloch School of Business and Public Administration at the University of Missouri-Kansas City.

WILLIAM H. DAVIDOW is general manager of the venture capital firm Mohr, Davidow Ventures in Menlo Park, California. The firm specializes in seed investments in high technology and biotechnology firms.

TERRENCE E. DEAL, Ph.D., is a Professor of Education in the Peabody College at Vanderbilt University.

JOHN H. EGGERS, Ph.D., heads the Entrepreneurial Leadership Initiative at the Center for Creative Leadership, San Diego, California.

EWING M. KAUFFMAN was the founder of Marion Laboratories, and Chairman and CEO of the Ewing Marion Kauffman Foundation. He passed away in 1993.

DENNIS P. KIMBRO, Ph.D., is director of the Center of Entrepreneurship at Clark-Atlanta University in Atlanta, Georgia.

ROBERT LAWRENCE KUHN, Ph.D., is president of the Geneva Companies in Irvine, California. The Geneva Companies specialize in mergers, acquisitions, and divestitures of privately held middle market businesses.

JANA B. MATTHEWS, Ph.D., is a senior research/teaching fellow and Director of Curriculum Development at the Center for Entrepreneurial Leadership Inc.

NEAL PATTERSON is Chairman and CEO of Cerner Corporation in Kansas City. Cerner designs information systems for healthcare institutions.

EDWARD PAYNE is president and CEO of Gateway Technologies, Inc., in Boulder, Colorado. Gateway assists companies in building strategic alliances for the transfer of proprietary technology to the chemical and textile industries.

ROBERT ROSEN, Ph.D., is the founder and president of Healthy Companies, a Washington, D.C. based, not-for-profit organization promoting organizational health as the key to America's social and economic success.

MICHIE P. SLAUGHTER is president of the Center for Entrepreneurial Leadership Inc. at the Ewing Marion Kauffman Foundation.

RAYMOND W. SMILOR, Ph.D., is vice president of the Center for Entrepreneurial Leadership Inc., and is the Marion Merrell Dow Distinguished Professor of Entrepreneurship at the Henry W. Bloch School of Business and Public Administration at the University of Missouri-Kansas City.

JOHN P. "JACK" STACK is president and CEO of Springfield Remanufacturing Corporation located in Springfield, Illinois. Springfield Remanufacturing specializes in the remanufacture of automotive and heavy duty equipment engines.

SPONSORS

THE CENTER FOR ENTREPRENEURIAL LEADERSHIP INC. at the Ewing Marion Kauffman Foundation was created by one of the country's most recognized entrepreneurs, the late Ewing M. Kauffman, founder of Marion Laboratories, former chairman of Marion Merrell Dow Inc., and owner of the Kansas City Royals baseball team.

The Center, a nonprofit educational institution, contributes to healthy economic communities by encouraging entrepreneurial leadership. In addition, by conducting applied research, developing innovative learning curricula for entrepreneurs, working through alliances, and nurturing the spirit of entrepreneurship in young people, the Center seeks to understand, support, and accelerate entrepreneurship in America.

THE HENRY W. BLOCH SCHOOL OF BUSINESS AND PUBLIC ADMINISTRATION at the University of Missouri-Kansas City is one of the region's leading urban schools of management. It offers accredited degree programs in business administration, accounting, and public administration, and an executive management program. The Bloch School's alliance with regional and national corporations and agencies adds a dimension of strength to management education in the area. The school is named for nationally known Kansas City entrepreneur, Henry W. Bloch, founder and chairman of H&R Block Inc.

EDITORS

DR. RAYMOND W. SMILOR, vice president of the Center for Entrepreneurial Leadership Inc. at the Ewing Marion Kauffman Foundation, is known nationally and internationally for his work and writing on entrepreneurship. In addition to holding the Marion Merrell Dow Chaired Professorship in Entrepreneurship at the Bloch School of Business at the University of Missouri-Kansas City, he served as executive director of the IC^2 Institute at the University of Texas at Austin before joining CEL, and has lectured in China, Japan, Europe, and Canada.

Dr. Smilor has published extensively with refereed articles appearing in numerous journals. He is author or editor of 10 books, including *Corporate Creativity* (Praeger, 1984), *Financing and Managing Fast-Growth Companies: The Venture Capital Process* (Lexington, 1985), *The Art and Science of Entrepreneurship* (Ballinger, 1987), and *Technology Transfer in Consortia and Strategic Alliances* (Rowman & Littlefield, 1992). In 1990 Dr. Smilor was selected as one of the Entrepreneurs of the Year and was inducted into the Entrepreneur of the Year Institute®.

DR. DONALD L. SEXTON, senior teaching and research fellow and director of applied research at the Ewing Marion Kauffman Foundation, was previously the William H. Davis Professor in the American Free Enterprise System at The Ohio State University, his doctoral and masters alma mater. Prior to joining Ohio State, he was the director of the Center for Entrepreneurship and the Caruth Professor of Entrepreneurship in the Hankamer School of Business at Baylor University. While at Baylor he established entrepreneurship majors at both the undergraduate and graduate level.

Dr. Sexton also spent 18 years in industry. He has coauthored eight books, the most recent being *Entrepreneurship: Creativity and Growth*. His efforts on behalf of entrepreneurship have earned him the Small Business Administration Certificate of Appreciation in 1981 and 1984, the SBA District and Regional Awards as the Innovation Advocate for 1982 and 1983, and the Freedoms Foundation's Leavey Award for Excellence in Private Enterprise Education in 1985. He is listed in *Who's Who in Finance & Industry* and *Who's Who in America*.

ISBN 1-56720-043-5

HARDCOVER BAR CODE